Frederick Currey, David Badham

A Treatise on the Esculent Funguses of England

Containing an Account of Their Classical History, uses, Characters...

Frederick Currey, David Badham

A Treatise on the Esculent Funguses of England
Containing an Account of Their Classical History, uses, Characters...

ISBN/EAN: 9783744783026

Printed in Europe, USA, Canada, Australia, Japan

Cover: Foto ©ninafisch / pixelio.de

More available books at **www.hansebooks.com**

A TREATISE

ON THE

ESCULENT FUNGUSES

OF

ENGLAND,

CONTAINING

AN ACCOUNT OF THEIR CLASSICAL HISTORY, USES, CHARACTERS,
DEVELOPMENT, STRUCTURE, NUTRITIOUS PROPERTIES,
MODES OF COOKING AND PRESERVING, ETC.

BY

CHARLES DAVID BADHAM, M.D.

EDITED BY FREDERICK CURREY, M.A., F.R.S., F.L.S.

Πολλὰ μὲν ἐσθλὰ μεμιγμένα πολλὰ δὲ λυγρά.—HOMER.

LONDON:
LOVELL REEVE & CO., HENRIETTA STREET, COVENT GARDEN.
1863.

PREFACE

TO THE SECOND EDITION.

My lamented friend Dr. Badham having died since the first publication of this work, my advice was asked upon the subject of the preparation of a new edition. It was wished that the text of the work should be altered as little as possible, and that the price of the book should be materially lessened. The latter object could not be effected without reducing the number of the Plates; but it appeared to me that some plates relating to details of structure might very well be omitted, as well as the figures of a few Italian species which, although interesting in themselves, are quite unnecessary in a book on British Esculent Fungi. With the exception of the omission of the description of these latter species, and the addition of the description of two other species hereafter referred to, the alterations in the text are too trifling to require notice. With regard to the Figures in this edition, most of them are those of the former plates, somewhat reduced; a few have been taken from the plates of Mr. Berkeley's 'Outlines of British Fungology,' and a few from original and other sources.

By a re-arrangement of the whole, the reduction in the number of the Plates has been effected, and, at the same time, figures of all the Fungi represented in the first edition have been given, as well as of two other species not there noticed.

I should observe, however, that by a mistake of the artist an extra figure of the Horse Mushroom has been inserted in Plate IV. instead of one of the Common Mushroom.

The two species above alluded to which were not figured in the first edition, are *Tuber æstivum* and *Helvella esculenta*. The former must have been inadvertently omitted by Dr. Badham, as it has long been known as abundant in certain parts of England. *Helvella esculenta*, although alluded to by Dr. Badham, was not at that time known to be a British species. It has since been observed near Weybridge in Surrey, where it occurs almost every spring. The plant figured in Pl. XV. fig. 6 of the first edition under the name of *Lycoperdon plumbeum*, is not that species, but *Lycoperdon pyriforme*; it will be found at Pl. VIII. fig. 5. Dr. Badham states that all puff-balls are esculent, but, judging from the smell of *Lycoperdon pyriforme*, I should much doubt whether it would make an agreeable dish. *Lycoperdon plumbeum* is now better known as *Bovista plumbea*, and *Lycoperdon Bovista* as *Lycoperdon giganteum*.

There is some confusion about the synonymy of the plants described by Dr. Badham as *Agaricus prunulus* and *Ag. exquisitus*. It is unnecessary to discuss the matter here, and I have thought it not desirable under the circumstances to alter Dr. Badham's nomenclature. They appear to be described in Mr. Berkeley's work as *Ag. gambosus*, Fr., and *Ag. arvensis*, Schæff.

Dr. Badham's observations on the spores of Fungi must be read in connection with the note added by him at the conclusion of the work; and to those who are interested in that part of the subject I should recommend the perusal of the seventh chapter of Mr. Berkeley's 'Outlines of British Fungology,' and Tulasne's recent work, 'Selecta Fungorum Carpologia.'

Mr. Cooke, in his 'Plain and Easy Account of British Fungi,' recently published, mentions some species as esculent which are not noticed in this work. I have however no experience of their qualities, and must refer the reader to Mr. Cooke's book for further information. He mentions Mr. Berkeley as an authority for considering *Agaricus rubescens* as suspicious; but, from long experience, I can vouch for its being not only wholesome, but, as Dr. Badham says, "a very delicate fungus."

F. C.

PREFACE

TO THE FIRST EDITION.

TO THE RIGHT REVEREND
THE LORD BISHOP OF NORWICH.

My Lord,

I had two reasons for desiring that this humble performance should appear under the sanction of your Lordship's name. Nothing could be more favourable to a Treatise on any department of Natural History, than the approval of one who has been so eminently successful in his cultivation of the same field.

But it is with much greater confidence that I dedicate a work, whose chief object it is to furnish the labouring classes with wholesome nourishment and profitable occupation, to a high functionary of that kingdom, which is distinguished from all others by recognizing the claims and furthering the interests of the poor.

I have the honour to be, my Lord,
With great respect, your Lordship's
Obliged and humble Servant,
C. D. BADHAM.

CONTENTS.

	Page
ETYMOLOGIES	1
THE RANGE OF FUNGUS GROWTHS	7
OF THEIR GENERAL FORMS, COLOURS, AND TEXTURE	10
ODOURS AND TASTES	13
EXPANSIVE POWER OF GROWTH	14
REPRODUCTIVE POWER	16
MOTION	16
PHOSPHORESCENCE	18
DIMENSIONS	18
CHEMICAL COMPOSITION	20
USES	21
MEDICAL USES	25
FUNGUSES CONSIDERED AS AN ARTICLE OF DIET	27
MODES OF DISTINGUISHING	40
CONDITIONS NECESSARY TO THEIR PRODUCTION	47
FAIRY RINGS	52
ON THE GROWTH OF FUNGUSES	53
ON THE DEVELOPMENT OF THE SPORES, OR QUASI-SEEDS*	58
OF THE ANNULUS, THE VELUM, AND THE VOLVA	66
OF THE STALK, AND OF THE PILEUS	68
OF THE GILLS, TUBES, PLAITS, AND SPINES	69
METHODICAL DISTRIBUTION OF BRITISH ESCULENT FUNGUSES	72
DESCRIPTION OF SPECIES:—	
Agaricus acris minor	120
Agaricus alutaceus	117
Agaricus atramentarius	111
Agaricus campestris	94
Agaricus castaneus	143
Agaricus comatus	112

* The word *seed* here, or wherever else introduced into the present work, is to be understood in its popular acceptation; correctly speaking, spores differ from seeds in the absence of an apparent embryo; but in a more catholic sense **spores are** seeds, since both are germinating granules, producing each after their **kind.**

CONTENTS.

DESCRIPTION OF SPECIES—*continued.*

	Page
Agaricus deliciosus	102
Agaricus Dryophilus	107
Agaricus emeticus	118
Agaricus exquisitus	100
Agaricus fusipes	141
Agaricus heterophyllus	113
Agaricus melleus	139
Agaricus nebularis	108
Agaricus Orcella	129
Agaricus oreades	106
Agaricus ostreatus	121
Agaricus personatus	105
Agaricus piperatus	141
Agaricus procerus	88
Agaricus prunulus	85
Agaricus ruber	115
Agaricus rubescens	123
Agaricus sanguineus	120
Agaricus semiglobatus	108
Agaricus ulmarius	140
Agaricus vaginatus	142
Agaricus violaceus	143
Agaricus virescens	116
Agaricus virgineus	145
Boletus edulis	90
Boletus luridus	104
Boletus scaber	103
Cantharellus cibarius	110
Clavaria coralloides	135
Fistulina hepatica	127
Helvella crispa	130
Helvella lacunosa	131
Helvella esculenta	131
Hydnum repandum	126
Lycoperdon Bovista	138
Lycoperdon plumbeum	136
Morchella esculenta	123
Morchella semilibera	124
Peziza acetabulum	133
Polyporus frondosus	133
Tuber æstivum	145
Verpa digitaliformis	132
CONCLUSION	146

DESCRIPTION OF PLATES.

Plate I.
Fig. 1. Agaricus prunulus.
 ,, 2. Agaricus personatus.

Plate II.
Agaricus procerus.

Plate III.
Fig. 1, 2. Boletus edulis.
 ,, 3, 4. Agaricus heterophyllus.

Plate IV.
Fig. 1. Polyporus frondosus.
 ,, 2. Agaricus nebularis.
 ,, 3, 4, 5. Agaricus exquisitus.

Plate V.
Fig. 1. Helvella lacunosa.
 ,, 2. Clavaria amethystina.
 ,, 3. Clavaria coralloides.
 ,, 4. Agaricus deliciosus.
 ,, 5. Clavaria cinerea.
 ,, 6. Clavaria rugosa.

Plate VI.

Fig. 1, 2. Boletus scaber.
 „ 3, 4, 5. Boletus luridus.

Plate VII.

Fig. 1, 2, 3. Agaricus comatus.
 „ 4. Agaricus oreades.
 „ 5. Agaricus Dryophilus.

Plate VIII.

Fig. 1. Cantharellus cibarius.
 „ 2. Tuber æstivum.
 „ 3, 4. Hydnum repandum.
 „ 5. Lycoperdon pyriforme.

Plate IX.

Fig. 1, 2. Agaricus atramentarius.
 „ 3. Agaricus melleus.

Plate X.

Agaricus ostreatus.

Plate XI.

Fig. 1, 2. Agaricus Orcella.
 „ 3, 4, 5. Agaricus rubescens.

Plate XII.

Fig. 1, 2. Fistulina hepatica.
 „ 3, 4, 5. Helvella esculenta.
 „ 6. Morchella esculenta.

INTRODUCTORY NOTICE.

No country is perhaps richer in esculent Funguses than our own; we have upwards of thirty species abounding in our woods. No markets might therefore be better supplied than the English, and yet England is the only country in Europe where this important and savoury food is, from ignorance or prejudice, left to perish ungathered.

In France, Germany, and Italy, Funguses not only constitute for weeks together the sole diet of thousands, but the residue, either fresh, dried, or variously preserved in oil, vinegar, or brine, is sold by the poor, and forms a valuable source of income to many who have no other produce to bring into the market. Well, then, may we style them, with M. Roques, "*the manna of the poor.*" To call attention to an article of commerce elsewhere so lucrative, with us so wholly neglected, is the object of the present work, to which the best possible introduction will be a brief reference to the state of the fungus market abroad.

The following brief summary was drawn up by Professor Sanguinetti, the Official Inspector ("*Ispettore dei Funghi*") at Rome; let it speak for itself:—" For forty days during the autumn, and for about half that period every spring, large quantities of Funguses, picked in the immediate vicinity of Rome, from Frascati, Rocca di Papa, Albano, beyond Monte Mario towards Ostia and the neighbourhood of the sites of Veii and Gabii, are brought in at the different gates. In the year 1837, the Government instituted the so-called *Congregazione Speciale di Sanità*, which, among other duties, was more particularly required to take into serious consideration the commerce of Funguses, from the unrestricted sale of which during some years past, cases of poisoning had not unfrequently occurred. The following decisions were arrived at by this body :—

"1st. That for the future an 'Inspector of Funguses,' versed in botany, should be appointed to attend the market in place of the peasant, whose supposed practical knowledge had been hitherto held as sufficient guarantee for the public safety.

"2nd. That all the Funguses brought into Rome by the different gates should be registered, under the surveillance of the principal officer, in whose presence also the baskets were to be sealed up, and the whole for that day's consumption sent under escort to a central depôt.

"3rd. That a certain spot should be fixed upon for the Fungus market, and that nobody, under penalty of fine and imprisonment, should hawk them about the streets.

"4th. That at seven o'clock A.M. precisely, the Inspector should pay his daily visit and examine the whole, the contents of the baskets being previously emptied on the ground by the proprietors, who were then to receive, if the Funguses were approved of, a printed permission of sale from the police, and to pay for it an impost of one baioccho (a halfpenny) on every ten pounds.

"5th. That quantities under ten pounds should not be taxed.

"6th. That the stale funguses of the preceding day, as well as those that were mouldy, bruised, filled with maggots, or dangerous (*muffi, guasti, verminosi, velenosi*), together with any specimen of the common mushroom (*Ag. campestris*) detected in any of the baskets, should be sent under escort and thrown into the Tiber.

"7th. That the Inspector should be empowered to fine or imprison all those refractory to the above regulations; and, finally, that he should furnish a weekly report to the Tribunal of Provisions (*Il Tribunale delle Grascie*) of the proceeds of the sale.

"As all fresh Funguses for sale in quantities *exceeding* ten pounds are weighed, in order to be taxed, we are enabled to arrive at an exact estimate of the number of pounds thus disposed of. The return of *taxed* Mushrooms in the city of Rome during the last ten years, gives a yearly average of between *sixty and eighty thousand pounds* weight; and if we double this amount, as we may safely do, in order to include such smaller *untaxed* supplies as are disposed of as bribes, fees, and presents, and reckon the whole at the rate of six baiocchi, or threepence per pound (a fair average), this will make the commercial value of fresh Funguses very apparent, showing it here to be little less than £2000 a year."

But the fresh Funguses form only a small part of the whole consumption, to which must be added the dried, the pickled, and the preserved; which sell at a much higher price than the first.* Supposing, however, that with these additions the supply of all kinds only reached a sum the double of that given above, even this would furnish us with an annual average of nearly *four thousand pounds sterling*; and this in a single city, and that, too, by no means the most populous one in Italy!† What, then, must be the net receipts of all the market-places of all the Italian States? For as in these the proportion of the price of esculent Funguses to butchers' meat is as two to three, it is plain that prejudice has deprived the poor of this country, not only of many thousand pounds of the former but also of as much of the latter, as might have

---

* At from twenty to thirty baiocchi, *i.e.* at about 1*s*. 3*d*. a pound.

† The population of Rome is only 154,000; that of Naples, 360,000; and that of Venice, 180,000.

been purchased by exchange, and of the countless sums which might have been earned in gathering them.*

* The Chinese present a striking contrast with ourselves in the care which they bestow on their esculent vegetation. "Some days since, M. Stanislas Julien presented to the Academy of Sciences, at Paris, a Chinese work, which merits a word or two of notice in the present circumstances of agricultural Europe. It is a treatise, in six volumes, with plates, entitled the 'Anti-Famine Herbal;' and contains the descriptions and representations of four hundred and fourteen different plants, whose leaves, rinds, stalks, or roots are fitted to furnish food for the people, when drought, ravages of locusts, or the overflow of the great rivers have occasioned a failure of rice and grain. Of this book the Chinese Government annually prints thousands, and distributes them gratuitously in those districts which are most exposed to natural calamities. Such an instance of provident solicitude on the part of the Chinese Government for the suffering classes may be suggestive here at home. A more general knowledge of the properties and capabilities of esculent plants would be an important branch of popular education."—*Athenæum*, Nov. 16, 1846.

ON THE

ESCULENT FUNGUSES

OF ENGLAND.

"Quos ipsa volentia rura
Sponte tulere sua carpsit."—*Virgil.*
"He culls from woods, and heights, and fields,
Those untaxed boons which nature yields."

ETYMOLOGIES.

By the word μύκης, ητος or ου, ὁ, whereof the usually received root, μῦκος (*mucus*), is probably factitious, the Greeks used familiarly to designate certain, but indefinite species of funguses, which they were in the habit of employing at table. This term, in its origin at once trivial and restricted to at most a few varieties, has become in our days classical and generic; Mycology, its direct derivative, including, in the language of modern botany, several great sections of plants (many amongst the number of microscopic minuteness), which have apparently as little to do with the original import of μύκης as smut, bunt, mould, or dry-rot, have to do with our table mushrooms. A like indefiniteness formerly characterized the Latin word *fungus*, though it be now used in as catholic a sense as that of μύκης; this, in the classic times of Rome, seems to have been confined (without any precise limitation, however) to certain sorts which might be eaten, and to others which it was not safe to eat. The

"Fungos colligit albos,"*

which occurs in Ovid's 'Fasti,' alludes to the former; the

"Sunt tibi boleti, fungos ego sumo suillos,"

of Martial, points to an inferior kind, but still esculent; whilst the word not unfrequently designated, if not actual toadstools, at least very equivocal mushrooms; of which character were those "ancipites fungi" presented by Veiento to his poor clients. Some melancholy etymologists, upon whom good mushrooms are really thrown away, would beget fungus out of *funus*, but Voss† judiciously rejects so harsh and forced a derivation, mentioning together with it others that are still more so.

The word *Boletus*, which now stands for a large genus of the section *Pileati*, was used in ancient Rome to designate that particular mushroom which had the honour, under Agrippina's orders and Locusta's cookery, of poisoning Claudius; in memory of which event it is now called *Amanita Cæsarea*, the Cæsar's mushroom. It occurs frequently both in the poets and prose writers of those days, and was in high esteem, as we collect from Pliny, who, though no mushroom-

* There are three kinds of esculent fungnses in Italy to which the epithet *albus* might apply, viz. the *Amanita alba*, of Persoon, the *Lycoperdon Bovista*, Linn. (or common puff-ball), and *Agaricus campestris*, Linn. (our common mushroom). The first kind grows in woods, and the second in dry uncultivated spots, whereas Ovid mentions these in conjunction with the Mallow (*Malva*), which grows in moist meadow-land; it is probable, therefore, that he here alludes to the *Pratajolo*, or meadow mushroom, or to that variety of it called from its whiteness "boule de neige."

† Etymol. *ad locum*.

fancier himself, calls this "Boletus optimi cibi." Nero, in playful allusion to his uncle's death, of which it was the occasion, designates it the 'food of gods,' βρῶμα θεῶν; and Martial celebrates it in many a convivial epigram; in one, for instance, where he asks his hard-hearted patron, "what possible pleasure it can be for his guests to sit at his table, and see him devour boletuses;" in another, "gold and silver and dresses may be trusted to a messenger, but not a boletus, (*subaudi*) because he will eat it on the way." This is the only ancient mushroom which we at once recognize by the description of it; "it originates," says Pliny, "in a volva, or purse, in which it lies at first concealed as in an egg; breaking through this, it rises upwards on its stalk; the colour of its cap is red; it takes a week to pass through the various stages of its growth and declension." The *suillus*—probably the same as the modern *porcino* (a word of analogous import), which was, and is, eaten by men as well as pigs, and not always by these*—was, according to Pliny, the fungus which most readily lent itself to poisoning by mistake; a remark so far consonant to modern experience, that it is liable, without some attention, to be confounded with the *Boletus luridus*, *B. cyanescens*, and others, which in their general shape and external hue resemble it, though it is not by any means certain that any of these species, with which it may be confounded, are themselves poisonous.† The word *tuber*, though it occasionally (as in Juvenal) meant the *truffle*, seems to have been used with considerable latitude. Thus

* Well-fed domestic pigs, on the authority o a friend, refuse it; but possibly, in the absence of full supplies of corn, they might be less dainty.

† Vittadini assures us that the "slips of dried boletus, sold on strings, are as frequently from these kinds as from the *Boletus edulis* itself; notwithstanding which, no accident was ever known to happen from the indiscriminate use of either."

the *tubers* said to spring up after those *optatos imbres*, those "long-wished-for showers of spring," were, probably, not truffles, but puff-balls, which, at the season of warm rains grow with incredible rapidity, forming an esteemed article of luxury, not only in Italy, but also in India; whereas the truffle never makes its appearance in the markets at such times, nor comes up so immediately after rain. *Tuber*, like our ancient "*fusseball*," seems a common appellation both for truffles and puff-balls. What the ancients understood by *hydnum* is as little precise or discriminate as the last word; for Theophrastus declares it to have a light bark, λειόφλοιον εἶναι, in which case it is a puff-ball, while the plant called ὑδνοφίλον, which is said to indicate the whereabouts of *hydna* in its neighbourhood, can only refer to the truffle. The truffle, however, which is now so much prized throughout Europe, seems not to have been known to the ancients, at least it is not described by them.* That which the Greeks called *misy*, and the Romans the Libyan truffle,† was white and of very delicious flavour, whilst by *hydnum* (when this word really meant truffle) they usually designated a particular kind bearing a smooth red rind, and abounding in certain districts of Italy; but having no chance against the black, nodulated *tuber tuberum*, the truffle *par excellence*, found in

* Dioscorides, who lived in the time of Nero, says that pigs dig up "truffles" in spring. Matthiolus, in his commentaries, speaks of an inferior, smooth-barked, red truffle known to the ancients, to which the above remark of Dioscorides perhaps applies; certainly it does *not* apply to the black truffle, which begins to come into the Roman market in November, and is over long before the spring.

† The Thracians are said to have intended this same *misy* under the new epithet of κεραύνιον, as though it were produced by thunder, unless indeed, as in Theoph. lib. i. cap. ix., we should read κρανίον, in which case they meant the *Lycoperdon giganteum*, a fungus frequently as big as, and in the form of, the human head: whence its name of *cranium*.

such abundance in the vicinities of Rome, Florence, Siena, etc., and, above all, amongst the Nursian hills of Umbria, over against Spoleto, whence it is largely exported throughout and beyond Italy. Under the name *Peziza*, the ancients appear at times to describe, unconsciously, a *Scleroderma* or species of puff-ball after it has evacuated its seed, when it presents a flattened surface, and so far looks like a *Peziza*, with which, in fact, it has no connection. By *Amanita*, Galen intended some kind of esculent fungus, but we know not which; this word has now come to have a more extensive import, and to designate, besides one or two species that are good, many of the most dangerous character. Whatever the ancient *Amanita* may have been, it was formerly in high repute; Galen declares that, next to the *Boletus*, it is ἀβλαβέστατον to eat—in which good report of it he is abundantly borne out by the concurrent testimony of Nicander. What Dioscorides meant by ἀγαρικὸν is another uncertainty, to resolve which we have not sufficient data; one thing seems plain, that it could not have been our officinal *Agaric*, for that grows upon the *Larch*, whereas his *Agaricon* grew upon the *Cedar*. Julius Scaliger amuses himself at the expense of Athenæus for saying that *Agaricus* is so called from the country of Agaria, whence he would make out that it originally came; whereas there never was such a country, his Agaria being, like our Poiatia, only another synonym for Fancy's fairyland.*

* Whoever has time to waste on the unprofitable speculations of the ancients concerning the parentage of funguses, and would like so to waste it, may consult Pliny, lib. xvi. cap. 8, lib. xxii. cap. 23; Hist. Nat. Dioscorides, lib. iii. cap. 78; Athenæus, lib. ii. in the Deipnosophisti; and after them Galen, Clusius, Portæ (Villæ, lib. x.), Imperato (Hist. Nat.), etc. The first really philosophical treatise which ascribes their origin, like that of other plants, to seeds, was published by Micheli, at Florence, in 1720.

The words *champignon* and *mushroom* have both a French origin, though, like the corresponding derivatives from the Greek and Latin, they too have come to signify things different from what they originally designated; *champignon*, for example, of which *champ* would seem to be the root, is *generic* in France. The 'Traités sur les Champignons' of Bulliard, Persoon, Paulet, Cordier, and Roques, are treatises of funguses *in genere;* whilst in England we restrict the word *champignon* to one small Agaric, which, as it grows in the so-called "fairy-rings," is hence named *Ag. oreades.* Again, there can be no doubt that our word *mushroom* (which, as contradistinguished from *toadstool,* is so far generic) comes from the French *mouceron* (originally spelt *mousseron*), and belongs of right to that most dainty of funguses, the *A. prunulus,* which grows amidst tender herbage and *moss* (whence its name), and which is justly considered, over almost the whole continent of Europe, as the *ne plus ultra* of culinary *friandise.* It abounds in various parts of England, being everywhere trodden underfoot, or reaped down, or dug up as a nuisance, while the rings which it so sedulously forms are as sedulously destroyed. The very odour which it exhales under these injuries, which the French call "un parfum exquis aromatisé,"* and the Italians, "un odore gratissimo,"† is in England occasionally cited to its disadvantage in confirmation of its supposed noxious qualities. Thus, while we use the word *mushroom,* which is the proper appellation of *this* species, for another (very good, no doubt, but wholly unlike it in its botanical characters, flavour, and appearance), this neglected, and ignorantly neglected, species, finds itself deprived of its rightful name, and proscribed as a toadstool. The origin of this last word, *toadstool,* which makes them seats or thrones

* Roques. † Vittadini.

for toads, does not quite satisfy me, I confess, though there be doughty authorities for it in Johnson's Dictionary and in Spenser's 'Faery Queen'!

> "The grisly todestool grown there mought I see,
> And loathed paddocks lording on the same;"

and, though an anonymous Italian authority declares that, in Germany, they have actually been seen sitting on their stools,* still, even in Germany, it must be admitted that they do not use them as frequently as we might expect, had they been created for this end. In that most grisly and ghastly waxwork exhibition at Florence, representing a charnel-house filled with the recent victims to a raging plague, in every stage of decomposition, the toad and his stool are not forgotten; but the artist, who had here to deal with matter, and to consult what it would bear, has not put his toads upon these brittle stools, lest, giving way, both should come to the ground; he has been content to convert them into toad-umbrellas, and to spread them as an awning over their heads.†

THE RANGE OF FUNGUS GROWTHS.

The family of Funguses, in the comprehensive sense in which we now employ the term, is immense. Merely catalogued and described, there are sufficient to fill an octavo volume of nearly 400 pages of close print, of British species alone; altogether, there cannot be less than 5000 recognized species at present known, and each year adds new ones to the list. The reader's surprise at this will somewhat diminish, when he considers, that not only the toadstools which beset his walks, whether

---

* 'Trattati dei Funghi.' Roma, 1804.

† Have not both the words *Tode* and the stool called after him some etymological, as they have undoubtedly a fanciful, connection with the word *tod*, death?

growing upon the ground or at the roots of trees, belong to this class, but that the immense hordes of parasites which feed at his expense, and foul, like the Harpies, whatever they may not actually consume, belong to it also.

For the single mushroom that we eat, how many hundreds there be that retaliate and prey upon us in return! To enumerate but a few, and these of the microscopic kinds (on the other side are some which the arms can scarcely embrace): the *Mucor mucedo*, that spawns upon our dried preserves; the *Ascophora mucedo*, that makes our bread mouldy ("mucidæ frustra farinæ"*); the *Uredo segetum*, that burns Ceres out of her own cornfields; the *Uredo rubigo*, whose rust is still more destructive; and the *Puccinia graminis*, whose voracity sets corn-laws and farmers at defiance, are all funguses! So is the grey *Monilia*, that rots, and then fattens upon, our fruits; and the *Mucor herbariorum*, that destroys the careful gleanings of the painstaking botanist. When our beer becomes mothery, the mother of that mischief is a fungus. If pickles acquire a bad taste, if ketchup turns ropy and putrifies, funguses have a finger in it all! Their reign stops not here; they prey upon each other; they even select their victims! There is the *Myrothecium viride*, which will only grow upon dry Agarics, preferring chiefly, for this purpose, the *Agaricus adustus*; the *Mucor†* *chrysospermus*, which

---

* Juvenal.

† Few minute objects are more beautiful than certain of these mucedinous *fungi fungorum*. A common one besets the back of some of the *Russulæ* in decay, spreading over it, especially if the weather be moist, like thin flocks of light wool, presenting on the second day a bluish tint on the surface. Under a powerful magnifier, myriads of little glasslike stalks are brought into view, which bifurcate again and again, each ultimate twig ending in a semilucent head, or button, at first blue, and afterwards black; which, when it comes to burst, scatters the spores, which are then (under the microscope) seen adhering to the sides of the delicate filamentary stalks like so many minute limpets.

attacks the flesh of a particular *Boletus;* the *Sclerotium cornutum,* which visits some other moist mushrooms in decay. There are some *Xylomas* that will spot the leaves of the Maple, and some those of the Willow, exclusively. The naked seeds of some are found burrowing between the opposite surface of leaves; some love the neighbourhood of burnt stubble and charred wood; some visit the sculptor in his studio, growing up amidst the heaps of moistened marble dust that have caked and consolidated under his saw. The *Racodium* of the low cellar* festoons its ceiling, shags its walls, and wraps its thick coat round our wine-casks,† keeping our oldest wine in closest bond; while the *Geastrum,* aspiring occasionally to leave this earth, has been found suspended, like Mahomet's coffin, between it and the stars, on the very highest pinnacle of St. Paul's.‡ The close cavities of nuts occasionally afford concealment to some species; others, like leeches, stick to the bulbs of plants, and suck them dry; these (the architect's and ship-builder's bane) pick timber to pieces, as men pick oakum; nor do they confine their selective ravages to plants alone, they attach themselves to animal structures,

---

* *Vide* the London Docks, *passim;* where he pays his unwelcome visits, and is in even worse odour than the exciseman.

† "Sir Joseph Banks having a cask of wine, rather too sweet for immediate use, he directed that it should be placed in a cellar, that the saccharine it contained might be more decomposed by age; at the end of three years he directed his butler to ascertain the state of the wine, when, on attempting to open the cellar-door, he could not effect it, in consequence of some powerful obstacle; the door was consequently cut down, when the cellar was found to be completely filled with a fungous production, so firm, that it was necessary to use an axe for its removal. This appeared to have grown from, or to have been nourished by, the decomposing particles of the wine, the cask being empty, and carried up to the ceiling, where it was supported by the fungus."—*Chambers's Journal.*

‡ Withering found one of these plants on the top of St. Paul's Cathedral; the first he had seen!

and destroy animal life; the *Onygena equina* has a particular fancy for the hoofs of horses and for the horns of cattle, sticking to these alone; the belly of a tropical fly* is liable, in autumn, to break out into vegetable tufts of fungous growth, and the caterpillar to carry about on his body a *Cordyceps* larger than himself. The disease called Muscadine, which destroys so many silkworms, is also a fungus (*Botrytis Bassiana*), which in a very short time completely fills the worm with filaments very unlike those it is in the habit of secreting.† The vegetating wasp,‡ too, of which everybody has heard, is only another mysterious blending of vegetable with insect life. Lastly, and to take breath, funguses visit the wards of our hospitals, and grow out of the products of surgical disease.§ Where, then, are they not to be found? do they not abound, like Pharaoh's plagues, everywhere? is not their name legion, and their province ubiquity?‖

OF THEIR GENERAL FORMS, COLOURS, TEXTURE, TASTES, SMELLS, ETC.

What geometry shall define their ever-varying shapes? who but a Venetian painter do justice to their colours?¶ or

---

* *Sporendonema Muscæ.*

† "When healthy caterpillars are placed within reach of a silkworm that has been destroyed by the Botrytis, they, too, contract the disease, and at last perish."—*Chambers's Journal*, October, 1845.

‡ A species of *Polystrix* is affected, whilst alive, with a parasitic kind of fungus, called *Sphæria*, which grows out of it, and feeds upon it.

§ Several of the French surgeons have given recitals of cases where, on removal of the bandages from sore surfaces, they have found a collection of funguses growing upon them, generally about the size of the finger (Lemery); one of them adds, that having reapplied the wrappings, a second batch came out in the course of twenty-four hours, and this for several days consecutively.

‖ For an accurate description of these funguses, the reader is referred to the excellent work of Mr. Berkeley.

¶ These, beautiful, but fleeting as beauty's blush, generally perish within a

what modifications of 'soft' and 'hard' convey an adequate knowledge of all their various crases and consistencies? As to shapes, some are simple threads, like the *Byssus*, and never get beyond this; some shoot out into branches, like seaweed; some puff themselves out into puff-balls; some thrust their heads into mitres;* these assume the shape of a cup,† and those of a wine-funnel;‡ some, like *A. mammosus*, have a teat; others, like the *A. clypeolarius*, are umbonated at their centre; these are stilted upon a high leg,§ and those have not a leg to stand on; some are shell-shaped, many bell-shaped, and some hang upon their stalks like a lawyer's wig;|| some assume the form of the horse's hoof, others of a goat's beard: in *Clathrus cancellatus* you look into the fungus through a thick red trellis which surrounds it. Some exhibit a nest in which they rear their young,¶ and, not to speak of those vague shapes,

> "If shapes they can be called, that shape have none
> Determinate,"

of such tree parasites as are fain to mould themselves at the will of their entertainer (the fate of parasites, whether under oak or mahogany), mention may be made of two, of which the forms are at once singular and constant; one exactly like an ear, and given for some good reason to Judas (*Auricula*

few hours; but I have seen some which, after a potting of 2000 years, retained their original hues unblemished, for they had been potted with the town of Pompeii, and are preserved with the other frescoes upon its walls.

* The *Mitrati* are not a very numerous class, of which the *Morel* may be taken as the type.

† The *Cupulati*, so called in consequence.

‡ *A. piperatus*.   § *A. procerus*.

|| *Agaricus comatus*, in allusion no doubt to which Plautus says of the Lord Chancellor of his day, "Fungino genere est, capiti se totum tegit,"—that his wig was so long as to hide his whole person.

¶ The *Nidularias* do so.

Judæ), clings to several trees, and trembles when you touch it; the other, which lolls out from the bark of chestnut-trees (*Lingua di Castagna*), is so like a tongue in shape and general appearance,* that in the days of enchanted trees you would not have cut it off to pickle or to eat on any account, lest the knight to whom it belonged should afterwards come to claim it of you. The above are amongst the most remarkable of the many Protean forms assumed by funguses; as to their colours, we find in one genus only species which correspond to every hue! The *Agaricus Cæsareus*, the *A. muscarius*, the *A. sanguineus*, assume the imperial purple, the *A. violaceus* a beautiful violet, the *A. sulphureus* a bright yellow, the *A. adustus* a dingy black, the *A. exquisitus*, and many others, a milk-white; whilst the *A. virescens* takes that which, in this class of plants, is the rarest of all to meet with, a pale-green colour. The upper surface of some is zoned with concentric circles of different hues; sometimes it is spotted, at other times of a uniform tint. The bonnets of some shine as if they were sprinkled with *mica*;† these have a rich velvety, those a smooth kid-like covering stretched over them. Some *pilei* are imbricated with brown scales, some flocked with white shreds of membrane, and some are stained with various-coloured milks secreted from within. The consistence of funguses is very different according to their sort, and the epithets of woody, corky, leathery, spongy, fleshy, gelatinous, pulpy, or mucous, will all find fitting application to some of them. Occasionally a fungus is secreted soft, but hardens by degrees into a compact and woody texture.

* The surface is rough with elevated papillæ, the structure fibrous, the flesh softly elastic, the colour bright red, looking like the tongue in the worst forms of gastro-enterite, with which its cold clammy surface when touched offers no correspondence.

† *A. micaceus*.

ODOURS AND TASTES.

Both one and the other are far more numerous in this class of plants than in any other with which we are acquainted. As to odours, though these be generally most powerful in the fresh condition of the fungus, they are sometimes increased by drying it, during which process too some species, inodorous before, acquire an odour, and not always a pleasant one. Some yield an insupportable stench; the *Phallus impudicus* and *Clathrus cancellatus* are of this kind. A botanist had by mistake taken one of the former into his bedroom; he was soon awakened by an intolerable fœtor, and was glad to open his window and get rid of it, as he hoped, and the *Phallus* together. Here he was disappointed; "sublatâ causâ non tollitur effectus," the fœtor remaining nearly the same for some hours afterwards. A lady, a friend of mine, who was drawing one in a room, was obliged to take it into the open air to complete her sketch. As to the *Clathrus*, I have found ten minutes in a room with it nine too many: it becomes insupportably offensive in a short time, and its infective stench has given rise to a superstition entertained of it throughout the Landes, viz. that it is capable of producing cancer—in consequence of which superstition the inhabitants, who call it Cancrou, or Cancer, cover it carefully over, lest by accident some one should chance to touch it, and become infected with that horrible disease in consequence.* Batsch has described an Agaric[†] of so powerful and peculiar a smell, that before he could finish his picture (for he was drawing it) a violent headache made him desist, "vehementi afficiebar capitis dolore." Of the others, some are graveolent in a savoury or in an unsavoury sense. This smells strong of onions,[‡] that of cinna-

---
* Thore.   † *Agaricus narcoticus*, Batsch, Fascic. vol. ii. pl. 81.
‡ *A. alliaceus.*

mon,* from which it takes its name; the *A. ostreatus* (*auct. nost.*) most powerfully of Tarragon; *A. odoratus,* and the *Cantharellus,* like apricots and ratafia (Purton); *Boletus salicinus,* "like the bloom of May" (Abbott); the *A. sanguineus,* when dry, savours of a stale poultice; *A. piperatus,* of the *Triglia,* or red mullet; the *Hydna* generally give out a smell of tallow; moulds have their own smells, which are mouldy and musty; some exhale the smell of putrid meat, many the odour of fresh meal; the spawn of *A. prunulus* and of the puff-balls (*Lycoperdons*) exhale an odour similar to the perfect plants; but the *Pietra funghaia,* filled with the spores of its own *Polyporus,* is without smell. When fresh, there is scarcely any perceptible odour in *Boletus edulis* or *B. luridus,* nor yet in the *A. Cæsareus* when recently gathered. A word about their tastes will suffice: with so many smells, they must needs have flavours to correspond, and so they have; sapid, sweet, sour, peppery, rich, rank, acrid, nauseous, bitter, styptic, might be all found in an English "gradus" (though at present, I am sorry to say, without any lines from poets in whose writings they occur), after the word 'Fungus.' In a few, generally of an unsafe character, there is little or no taste in the mouth while they are being masticated, but shortly after deglutition, the fauces become dry, and a sense of more or less constriction is apt to supervene, which frequently continues for some time afterwards.

EXPANSIVE POWER OF GROWTH.

Soft and yielding as vegetable structures appear to the touch, the expansive force of their growth is almost beyond calculation. The effects of this power, of which the experience of every one will furnish him with some instances, are perhaps

* *A. cinnamomeus.*

nowhere more strikingly exemplified than amidst the ruins of **its own creation**. Coeval with **many old** brick fabrics of earlier times, perhaps embedded in the very mortar which holds them **together, it** may lurk **there for** centuries in quiescence, till once **arousing** its energies, it continues to exert them in ceaseless activity ever after. **It has at** Rome planted its pink Valerians on her highest towers, and its wild fig-tree in the **breaches of** her **walls;** nor are the granite obelisks of her piazzas, **nor** the **classic groups** in marble on her **Quirinal mount, entirely** exempt **from its encroachments.** A conspiracy of plants, *one hundred strong*, have long ago planned the destruction of the Coliseum; **their** undermining process advances each year, and neither iron nor new brickwork can **arrest it** long. That old Roman cement, which the barbarians gave up as impracticable, and the pickaxe of the Barberini had but begun to disintegrate, will, **ere the lapse of another** century, be effectually pulled to pieces by the **rending arm of** vegetation. Here, as erst in Juvenal's time, **the *mala ficus*** finds no walls too **strong to rive asunder, no tower beyond the** reach of its scaling, no monument too **sacred for it to touch.** In the class of plants immediately **under** consideration, while **the expansive** effort **of growth is equal to** what it is in other **cases, its effects are far more startling from** their suddenness. M. Bulliard (to cite one or two instances out of a great **many) relates, that on placing a** *Phallus impudicus* within a **glass vessel, the** plant **expanded so rapidly** as to shiver its **sides with an** explosive detonation **as loud** as that of a pistol. **Dr. Carpenter, in his** 'Elements of Physiology,' mentions that "**in the** neighbourhood **of Basingstoke a** paving-stone, measuring **twenty-one inches square, and weighing eighty-three** pounds, was **completely raised an inch and a half out of its** bed by a mass **of toadstools, of from six to seven inches in** diameter, and that nearly the whole pavement of the town suffered displacement from the same cause." A friend has seen a crop of puff-balls raise large flagstones considerably above the plane of their original level; and I have myself recently witnessed an extensive displacement of the pegs of a wooden pavement which had been driven nine inches into the ground, but were heaved up irregularly, in several places, by small bouquets of Agarics, growing from below.

REPRODUCTIVE POWER.

Funguses have a remarkable power of re-forming such parts of their substance as have been accidentally or otherwise removed. Vittadini found that when the tubes of a *Boletus* were cut out from a growing plant, they were after a time reproduced. Where deep holes have been eaten into these plants by snails, such holes, on the *Boletus* attaining to its full growth, are partially refilled. If the tender *Polyporus* be cut across, the wound immediately sets about healing by the first intention, leaving not even a cicatrice to mark the original seat of the injury. The *Lycoperdons* (*Bovista*), which are often accidentally wounded by the scythe, have the same faculty of repairing the injury, remodelling afresh the parts that may have been excised from them.*

MOTION.

In a recent work on 'Insect Life,' I have discoursed somewhat at large on the insufficiency of any kind of movements as proofs of sensation, quoting, amidst other evidences to this effect, certain remarkable movements in plants. Some of the present family exhibit the phenomena of insensitive motion in a remarkable manner, and might have been added to the

* Fries.

list already cited in that publication. Mr. Robson has given us a very interesting account of the movements he observed in the scarlet *Clathrus*, which is here transcribed in his own words. It is interesting to notice how an unbiassed observer uses the very terms to designate the movements of a plant which would have been minutely descriptive of those of an insect:—" At first I was much surprised to see a part of the fibres, that had got through a rupture in the top of the *Clathrus*, moving like the legs of a fly when laid on his back. I then touched it with the point of a pin, and was still more surprised when I saw it present the appearance of a little bundle of worms entangled together, the fibres being all alive. I next took the little bundle of fibres quite out, and the animal motion was then so strong as to turn the head halfway round, first one way and then another, and two or three times it got out of the focus. Almost every fibre had a different motion; some of them twined round one another, and then untwined again, whilst others were bending, extending, coiling, waving, etc. The fibres had many little balls adhering to their sides, which I take to be the seeds, and I observed many of them to be disengaged at every motion of the fibres; the seeds appeared like gunpowder finely granulated." Instances from other authors abound. " An *Helvella inflata*, on being touched by me once, threw up its seeds in the form of a smoke, which arose with an elastic bound, glittering in the sunshine like particles of silver."* "The *Vibrissea truncorum*, taken from water and exposed to the rays of the sun, though at first smooth, is soon covered with white geniculated filaments, which start from the *hymenium*, and have an oscillating motion."† The *Pilobolus*, of which so accurate an account has been given us by the great Florentine mycologist,‡ casts,

* Bolton. † Persoon. ‡ Micheli.

as its name imports, its seeds into the air; these also escape with a strong projectile force from the upper surface of Pezizas, the anfractuosities of the Morel, and from the gills of Agarics.*

PHOSPHORESCENCE.

Several kinds of funguses, and the spawn of the truffle, emit a phosphorescent light; of the first, the *Agaricus olearius*, not uncommon in Italy, is sometimes seen at night, feebly shining amidst the darkness of the olive grove. The coal-mines near Dresden have long been celebrated for the production of funguses which emit a light similar to a pale moonlight. Mr. Drummond describes an Australian fungus with similar properties; and another very interesting one, an Agaric, is noticed by Mr. Gardner, in his 'Travels in Brazil.'†

DIMENSIONS.

Most funguses do not present great anomalies in their size,

---

* These last, placed in a wineglass, over a sheet of white paper, frequently disperse the seminal dust over a ring of twice the natural dimensions of the Agaric.

† "One dark night, about the beginning of December, while passing along the streets of the Villa de Natividade, I observed some boys amusing themselves with some luminous object, which I at first supposed to be a kind of large fire-fly; but, on making inquiry, I found it to be a beautiful phosphorescent fungus, belonging to the genus *Agaricus*, and was told that it grew abundantly in the neighbourhood, on the decaying leaves of a dwarf palm. Next day I obtained a great many specimens, and found them to vary from one to two and a half inches across. The whole plant gives out at night a bright phosphorescent light, of a pale greenish hue, similar to that emitted by the larger fire-flies, or by those curious, soft-bodied, marine animals, the *Pyrosomæ*; from this circumstance, and from growing on a palm, it is called by the inhabitants 'Flor do Coco;' the light given out by a few of these fungi in a dark room, was sufficient to read by. It proved to be quite a new species, and, since my return from Brazil, has been described by the Rev. M. J. Berkeley under the name of *Agaricus Gardneri*, from preserved specimens which I brought home."—*Travels in the Interior of Brazil*, 1846.

but retain nearly the same dimensions throughout the whole course of their being; some few species, however, seem to have a faculty of almost indefinite expansion. The usual size of a puff-ball, as we all know, is not much larger than an egg, but some puff-balls attain to the dimensions of the human head,* or exceed it. Mr. Berkeley quotes the case of a *Polyporus squamosus*, which in three weeks grew to seven feet five inches in periphery, and weighed thirty-four pounds; also of a *Polyporus fraxineus*, which in a few years measured forty-two inches across. Clusius† tells us of a fungus in Pannonia, of such immense size, that after satisfying the cravings of a large mycophilous household, enough of it remained to fill a chariot; this must have been the *Polyporus frondosus*, to which *Polyporus* John Bapt. Porta‡ also alludes as that called *gallinace*§ by the Neapolitans, which is so big, he says, that you can scarcely make your hands meet round it, "brachiis diductis vix homo complecti possit;" he had known it attain twelve pounds weight in a few days.‖ Bolton,

* Hence it was called κρανίον (vide Theoph. Lib. vol. i. cap. 9) by the ancients. Cesalpinus describes it under the name of *Peziza*, and reports that it is common in the woods of Pisa, whence men gather to eat them. We read also, in an ancient Italian writer (Cicinelli), that the environs of Padua produce enormous puff-balls, of which one (unless this author was given to *puffing*) measured not less than two feet across, in one direction, being upwards of a foot and a half in its least diameter. It was big enough, he says, to have written on its rind the celebrated inscription attributed by Dion Cassius to the Dacians, which they presented to the Emperor, "in quo scriptum erat Latinis literis Burros sociosque omnes cum hortari ut domum reverteretur pacemque coleret." Other authors also (Alph. de Tuberibus,—not truffles, but puff-balls,—cap. xvii.; Imperato, Hist. Nat. Hol. vol. xxvii. cap. 5) speak of puff-balls of sixty and one hundred pounds weight.

† Hist. Plant. vol. ii. p. 275.

‡ Villæ, Lib. vol. x. cap. 80.

§ By this word, however, the vulgar generally understood the *Cantharellus cibarius*.

‖ This species, which is somewhat rare in England, occurred in abundance

in 1787, found an *Agaricus muscarius*, which, "after the removal of a considerable portion of its stalk, weighed nearly two pounds;" Withering, an *A. Georgii*, "which weighed fourteen pounds," and Mr. Stackhouse another of the same species in Cornwall, "which was eighteen inches across, and had a stem as thick as a man's wrist;" and I lately picked in the park at Buckhurst, a *Boletus edulis* which measured twenty-eight inches round its pileus, and eight round the stem, and a few days later a *B. pachypus*, the girth of which was thirty-two inches.

CHEMICAL COMPOSITION.

Of all vegetable productions these are the most highly azotized, that is, animalized in their composition—a fact not only evinced by the strong cadaverous smell which some of them give out in decay, and by the savoury animalized meat which others afford at table, but on the evidence of chemistry also. Thus Dr. Marcet has proved that, like animals, they absorb a large quantity of oxygen, and disengage in return, from their surface, a large quantity of carbonic acid; all however do not exhale carbonic acid, but, in lieu of it, some give out hydrogen, and others azotic gas. They yield, moreover, to chemical analysis the several components of which animal structures are made up; many of them, in addition to sugar, gum, resin, a peculiar acid called fungic acid, and a variety of salts, furnish considerable quantities of *albumen*, *adipocire*, and *osmazome*, which last is that principle

---

this year (1847) in the neighbourhood of Tunbridge Wells. I found four specimens of it on the oak-roots in the Grove, one of which rose nearly a foot from the ground, measured considerably more than two and a half feet across, and weighed from eighteen to twenty pounds; the other specimens were of much smaller dimensions.

that gives its peculiar flavour to meat gravy. The *Polyporus sulphureus* is frequently covered with little crystals of the binoxalate of potash;* the *Agaricus piperatus* yields the acetate of potash,† and it is probable that other funguses of which we have as yet no recorded analysis will, on the institution of such, be found to contain some new and unexpected ingredient peculiar to themselves. When these several substances have been duly extracted from funguses, there is left behind for a common base the solid structure of the plant itself; this, which is called *fungine*, is white, flabby, insipid in its taste, but highly nutritious in its properties. If nitric acid be poured upon it, an immediate disengagement of azotic gas takes place, and several new substances are the result: a bitter principle, a reddish resinoid matter, hydrocyanic and oxalic acids, and two remarkable fatty substances, whereof one resembles tallow, the other wax. If dilute sulphuric acid be poured upon this fungine, no change ensues; but if muriatic acid be substituted, the result is a jelly.

USES.

The uses to which funguses have been put are various, and, had the properties of these plants been as extensively investigated as those which belong to the phanerogamic classes, they would probably by this time have proved still more numerous: some, as the *Polyporus sulphureus*, furnish a useful colour for dyeing;‡ the *Agaricus atramentarius* makes ink; divers Lycoperdons, of which other mention will be made presently when we come to speak of such species as are esculent, have also been employed for stupefying bees, for stanching blood, and for making tinder; their employment in the first of these capacities, seems to have escaped the

* Robert Scott, Act. Linn. Soc. vol. viii. p. 202. † Dufresnoy. ‡ Roques.

observation of the accurate author of 'Les Jardins,' who has mentioned the others:—

> "Ce puissant Agaric, qui du sang épanché
> Arrête les ruisseaux, et dont le sein fidèle
> Du caillou pétillant recueille l'étincelle."

The 'caillou,' alas, like the poet who struck this spark out of it, is now obsolete; but *amadou* is still in vogue, being employed for many household purposes; in addition to which, a medical practitioner of Covent Garden has of late been in the habit of using extensive sheets of it to cover over and protect the backs of those bedridden invalids whose cruel sufferings make such large demands upon our sympathy,—for the alleviation of which so little is to be done!—as it is more elastic than chamois leather, it is less liable to crumple up when lain upon, and on this account has been preferred to it by several of our metropolitan surgeons of eminence; some employ it also as a gentle compress over varicose veins, where it supports the distended vessels without pressing too tightly upon the limb. Gleditsch relates, that the poorer inhabitants of Franconia stitch it together, and make dresses of it; and also that the Laplanders burn it in the neighbourhood of their dwellings, to secure their reindeer from the attacks of gadflies, which are repelled by the smoke; thus "good at need," it really deserves the epithet of 'puissant,' given to it by Delille.*

* *Amadou* is largely used in Italy, where it is called *esca*; the Latins likewise knew it by this name, though their more common appellation for it was *fomes*; the Byzantine Greeks hellenicized *esca* into ὕσκα, which was their word for it; the ancient Greeks called it ζώπυρον. Salmasius tells us how it used to be made in his time, which indeed was the same as now: the fungus was first boiled, then beaten to pieces in a mortar, next hammered out to deprive it of its woody fibres, and lastly, being steeped in a strong solution of nitre, was left to dry in the sun. It appears, on the testimony of the anonymous author of the article "Fungo" in the 'Dizionario Classico di Medicina,'

The *Polyporus squamosus* makes a razor-strop far superior to any of those at present patented, and sold, with high-sounding epithets, far beyond their deserts. To prepare the *Polyporus* for this purpose, it must be cut from the ash-tree in autumn, when its juices have been dried and its substance has become consolidated; it is then to be flattened out for twenty-four hours in a press, after which it should be carefully rubbed with pumice, sliced longitudinally, and every slip that is free from the erosions of insects be then glued upon a wooden stretcher. Cesalpinus knew all this! and the barbers in his time knew it too;* and it is not a little remarkable that so useful an invention should, in an age of puffing, advertisement, and improvement, like our own, have been entirely lost sight of. Imperato employed and recommends it as an excellent detergent, with which to brush and comb out the scurf from the hair.

The *Agaricus muscarius* is largely employed in Kamtchatka, in decoction with the *Epilobium angustifolium*, as an intoxicating liquor.† The Laplanders smear it on the walls and bedposts of their dwellings, to destroy bugs (Linn.); and

that it is also eaten when young; but I cannot speak of it from personal experience:—" In prima età mangiasi colto di fresco affettato e condito d'ogni modo; specialmente nelle provincie di Belluno ed Udine, o salasi per la quadragesima."

* " Di questo fungo servavanosene i barbieri in cambio delle strugghie dette più volgaremente *codette*, atte a far riprendere il perduto filo a loro rasoi."

† "This is the 'Moucho more' of the Russians, Kamtchadales, and Koriaks, who use it for intoxication; they sometimes eat it dry, but more commonly immersed in a liquor made from the *Epilobium*, and when they drink this liquor, they are seized with convulsions in all their limbs, followed with that kind of raving which accompanies a burning fever. They personify this mushroom, and, if they are urged by its effects to suicide, or any other dreadful crime, they pretend to obey its commands; to fit themselves for premeditated assassination they recur to the use of the Moucho more."—*Rees's Cyclopædia*, art. "*Agaric.*"

Clusius relates, that it is sold extensively in the market at Frankfort, to poison flies; for this purpose, it is either cut into small pieces and thrown about the premises, or else boiled in milk and placed upon the window-sills; in either case it is vastly inferior in efficacy to that celebrated "mort aux mouches," the impure oxide of cobalt, that is, to the arsenic which this contains. The above are a few of the uses, exclusive of the esculent or medical ones, to which funguses have been put; it is fair, however, to notice that they maintain a debtor, as well as a creditor, account with mankind, in which the balance seems to be occasionally quite against us; those that are most injurious are generally, as has been already stated, of the microscopic kinds; whereof some attack young plants still underground, emulging them completely of their juices, in consequence of which they perish; others, like the corn-blights, permit the plant to attain maturity before they begin their work of destruction, and destroy it just as it is beginning to fructify.* The fearful epidemics to which grain so infected has given rise are well known, though it is still a matter of question whether the ergoted corn owes its unwholesome qualities to the injury which it had sustained from the blight, or to the blight itself. Though the mischief produced by parasitic funguses be unquestionably great, this occasional and very partial evil is more than compensated by the much greater amount of good accomplished solely by their agency, in the assistance they afford to the decomposition of animal and vegetable tissues, which has procured for them the name, not unaptly applied, of "nature's scavengers."

* In such cases the minute fungus is probably absorbed *in ovo* and disseminated with the sap through the plant; as this ascends from the root, it remains undeveloped however till the corn is in ear, at which time it finds in the nascent grain the necessary conditions for its own development.

This decomposition they effect by assimilating, through the medium of their radicles, the juices of the decaying structure in which they are developed, loosening thereby its cohesion, and causing it to break up into a rapid dissolution of its parts.*

MEDICAL USES.

Of the funguses formerly employed in medicine few are now in vogue; the ergot of rye still keeps its ground, and in cases of protracted labour, when judiciously employed, is valuable in assisting nature when unequal to the necessary efforts of parturition. Another fungus, formerly much in fashion, though now put on the shelf, seems really to deserve further trial; I mean the *Polyporus suaveolens* (Linn.), which in that most intractable disease, tubercular consumption, surely claims to be tried when there are such respectable authorities to vouch for its surprising effects, in cases where everything else had been notoriously unsuccessful.† Sartorius was the first to prescribe it as a remedy in phthisis, and its employment with this view, since his day, has at various times been præconized on the Continent; the dose generally recommended being a scruple of the powder two or three times a day. Of the cases published by Professors Schmidel and Wendst (which have an air of good faith in their recital, well entitling them to consideration), I abridge one as an example, though the others are not less interesting; and

---

* The mischief thus produced by dry-rot may be arrested by steeping the affected timber in a solution of corrosive sublimate, which, forming a chemical union with the juices of the woody fibre, prevents their being abstracted by the dry-rot, that would else have maintained itself and spread at their expense.

† A reputation that revives may not be so good as one that survives, but the very fact of such revival shows that the good opinion formerly entertained was not altogether groundless.

while it is certainly to be regretted that the absence of stethoscopic indications should prevent our having any positive evidence as to the precise condition of the diseased lung, or of the nature of the secretion expectorated, still, even supposing them to be simple cases of chronic bronchitis, with marasmus the efficacy of the remedy is scarcely less striking or instructive. "A young man, ætat. twenty-one, was seized at the beginning of autumn with inflammatory cough and hæmoptysis, which were partially subdued by V. S. and the ordinary antiphlogistic treatment; but the cough, coming on again with renewed severity during the winter, was accompanied with the expuition of glairy mucus, which was sometimes specked with blood. Towards the spring the young man had become much thinner, and was continuing to waste away; the expectoration also had changed its colour, and had become fetid and green; his nights were feverish and disturbed; he had no desire for food, and ate but little; his ankles had begun to swell; he had copious night-sweats and diarrhœa. A teaspoonful of an electuary of the *P. suaveolens* in honey was given him three times a day, and *nothing else;* and, extraordinary as it may appear, under this treatment the sweats speedily began to diminish with the cough, and after a three months' continuance of the medicine the patient entirely recovered."*

The *Polyporus laricis*, the so-called Agaric of pharmacy, is a powerful but most uncertain medicine, and has been also recommended in consumption. I once administered a few grains of it in this disease, when violent pains and hypercæ-

---

* Enslin was in the habit of uniting this *Polyporus* with Peruvian Bark, and obtained from it the happiest results: "Omnium mihi arridet connubium ejus cum cortice Peruviano"—to which "connubium," no doubt, some of its good effects are to be attributed.

tharsis supervened, which lasted for several hours. MM. B. Lagrange and Braconnot found it to contain a large quantity of an acrid resin, to which it no doubt owes its hypercathartic properties. To judge from this single case, which, however, tallies with the experience of others, I should say that this fungus was, in medicine, to be looked upon as a very suspicious ally.* The *A. muscarius* has also been used in medicine. Whistling, so long ago as 1778, wrote on its healing virtues, in Latin, recommending its powder as a valuable application with which to sprinkle sanious sores and excoriated nipples. Plenck gave drachm doses of it internally in epilepsy, and, together with Bernhard and Whistling, attests its success. It appears that the *Phallus mucus* in China, and the *Lycoperdon carcinomale* near the Cape of Good Hope, are used also by the inhabitants of those countries as external applications for cancerous sores. The *Phallus*, rubbed upon the skin, is said to deaden its sensibility, like the *narke*, or electric skate.

FUNGUSES CONSIDERED AS AN ARTICLE OF DIET.

If all the good things ever said about the stomach since the days of Menenius Agrippa, or before his time, could be collected, they would doubtless form an interesting volume; Arctæus has somewhere quaintly, but not unaptly, called it the "house of Plato;" in another place he speaks of it as the "seat" (as if κατ' ἐξοχὴν) "of pleasure and of pain;" and so it is indeed, and it has moreover a notorious tendency, when provoked, to cool our charity and to heat our blood; its

---

* Haller relates, that the inhabitants of Piedmont are in the habit of swallowing a small piece of this Agaric, when they have drunk with their water some of those small leeches in which it abounds. Bomare mentions of this same Agaric, that the inhabitants of Baleu use it in powder to heal blains in their cattle.

sympathies by nervous attachments, both of "continuity" and of "contiguity,"* with the other organs of the body, are extensive and complicated; no wonder then that it should have enlisted ours in its behalf, and that few of us would offend it wittingly, though by indiscretions we do offend it continually.

In the "sensual philosophy," of the French school particularly, the stomach has received marked attention, ranking in that country as the most noble of the *viscera*.† Even in those republican times when no other rights were held sacred throughout France, the privileges of the stomach were respected; when men found that they might get on quite as well, or better, with a bad heart, but that they could not get on so well without a good digestion, it is not so much to be wondered at if they made idols of their bellies, established a School of Cooks to rival the School of Athens, and became famous for "those charming little suppers in which they used to set the decencies of life at defiance."‡ But if in France far too much attention has been paid to the culinary art, too little attention has surely been paid to it at home; for the art of cookery, properly understood, is not only the art of pleasing the palate, but the stomach also.§ In France, the dinner is the thought of the morning, and sometimes the business of the day, but in France everybody dines; in England, where the word 'dinner' never occurs till it is announced,

---

* Hunter.

† It is the Frenchman's *heart!* "J'ai mal au cœur" means, as every one knows, in the French tongue, not 'I am sick at heart,' as it professes to say, but 'I am sick at stomach'!

‡ Walpole.

§ The phrase "I like it, but it does not like me," which one sometimes hears at table, having a reference to some particular idiosyncrasy of the party who makes the remark, does not invalidate the truth of this general proposition.

a few wealthy men dine well, the middling ranks badly, and the poor not at all. Not that even the poorer orders generally want the necessary materials for such repast; they frequently consume more butcher's meat than is consumed by their Continental neighbours; it is simply that they want skill in preparing it. If it be scanty, they cannot tell how to make the most of it; if it be homely, they cannot tell how to improve its flavour by uniting and blending with it a certain class of inexpensive luxuries, which, though they grow everywhere throughout the country, are everywhere neglected. Touching the wholesomeness or unwholesomeness of these, I have now a few words to address to the common-sense reader; that is, to him who prefers feasting upon funguses to fasting out of mere prejudice. Formerly men used to refer such questions as this to their physician; they would

"Try what Mead or Cheselden advised."*

intending, perhaps, to take some little poetical license with it afterwards. Abernethy, on the anecdote of the oysters and oyster-shells being duly substantiated, would have been *ostracized* from polite society in those days of decorous etiquette, when, as medical men affected to be more *dientereumatic* with the insides of their patients than any of us now pretend to be, they must needs have been far more affable when consulted on such cases than we of the present day might be; though they did not therefore always answer the same question in the same way; one, for instance, "Le médecin Tant Pis," would frequently *proscribe* the very things that his rival, "Le médecin Tant Mieux," had just been recommending. When men

* Pope. Mead, if anybody, ought to have been good authority on the subject of this particular diet. He had written, *ex professo*, upon poisons; and the Florentine mycologist Micheli had dedicated several newly-discovered funguses to him. He was therefore both a Toxicologist and a Mycologist.

came to find they must either give up some favourite article of food or else give up the anathema pronounced against it, they generally preferred the latter course, and were sure, to use a medical phrase, to " do well" if they did so; whilst a few wretched hypochondriacs, adopting the other alternative, and living strictly *en régime*, became only the more hypochondriacal for their pains.

None but a determined theorist* would nowadays think of prescribing diet for the stomach of a single patient, far less for all those of a polygastric public; neither does an enlightened, self-educated public, that can read Liebig and thoroughly appreciate its own case, hold out much encouragement for such advice. The day is past without return for long-winded prose epic on indigestion; a livelier mode of dealing with the subject of *non-naturals*, in the shape of novels and romances, has won the public ear. Broussais' five-act tragedy of 'Gastro-Enteritis'† has received its last plaudits; already has Crabbe's *euthanasia* to this class of authors attained its full accomplishment:—

> " Ye tedious triflers, Truth's destructive foes,
> Ye sons of Fiction clad in stupid prose,
> O'erweening teachers, who, yourselves in doubt,
> Light up false fires and send us far about,

---

* " No thought too bold, no airy dream too light,
That will not prompt your Theorist to write;
No fact so stubborn, and no proof so strong,
Will e'er convince him he *could* argue wrong."—*Crabbe.*

† Broussais divides inflammatory dyspepsia into *five* parts or acts. That Leach of leeches, whose word once passed for more than it was worth, came at last to see himself and his *sangsues* utterly abandoned, and to have the mortification of lecturing in his old age to empty benches. " Quantum mutatus ab illo " of less than twenty years before, and who had been the cause of as much innocent bloodshedding as Napoleon himself, and used to kill his patients that his leeches might be fed!

> Long may the spider round your pages spin,
> Subtle and slow, her emblematic gin.
> Buried in dust and lost in silence dwell,
> Most potent, dull, and reverend friends, farewell!"

No article of diet was ever half so roughly handled as the fungus. What diatribes against it might be cited from the works of Athenæus, Dioscorides, Galen, Pliny, the Arabian physicians, and all their commentators! What terrible recitals, too, of poisoning from some few species have been industriously circulated, and the unfavourable inference drawn from these, been applied to the whole tribe—a mistake which some writers, even in modern times, have perpetuated. Thus, Kirker votes the whole " a family of malignants;"* thus too Allen and Batarra pen unsolicited *apages*,† and warn us, in an especial manner, to beware of them; while Scopoli includes in his very definition of a fungus, that it is of a class of plants which are always to be suspected, and which are for the most part poisonous. Tertullian, with more of epigram than of truth, makes out, that for every different hue they display there is a pain to correspond to it, and just so many modes of death as there are distinct species;‡ to all which, and a great deal more similar rhapsody and invective, tens of thousands of our Continental neighbours in the daily habit of eating nothing else but funguses might reply, in the words of Plautus—

> "Adeone me fuisse *fungum* ut qui illis crederem?"

Those who abuse funguses generally do so from prejudice rather than from personal experience, objecting to their flesh as being heavy of digestion, and to their juices as being more

---

* "Fungus qualiscunque sit semper *malignus*."—*Kirker, Lab. de Pest.*
† "*Apage* ergo perniciosa isthæc gulæ blandimenta."
‡ "Quot colores tot dolores, quot species tot pernicies."

or less prejudicial to health. Some say they are too rich, others of too heating a character. These objections are for the most part without foundation, as those who eat them can abundantly testify. To quote the authority of one or two medical friends on the Continent, formed on large personal experience, in favour of the excellence of this diet, Professors Puccinelli of Lucca, Briganti of Naples, Sanguinetti of Rome, Ottaviani of Urbino, Viviani of Genoa, are all consumers of funguses. Vittadini, whose excellent work on the esculent kinds of Italy is without a rival, himself eats, and gives us ample receipts for dressing them. In France, a similar service has been rendered to the public by Paulet, Persoon, Cordier, and Roques,* who have severally published excellent treatises on the various kinds fit for food, as they occur in the different provinces; whilst the influence of the last winter has been the means of introducing several new species into the Parisian markets, thus causing them to be very generally known. Not to multiply individual testimony needlessly, let that of Schwægrichen suffice, who tells us, that on seeing the peasants about Nuremberg eating *raw* mushrooms,† he too, for several weeks, restricted himself entirely to this diet, "eating with them nothing but bread, and drinking nothing but water, when, instead of finding his health impaired, he rather experienced an increase of strength." *Vegetior evasit!* as the inscription at Rome relates to have been the case with

---

* M. Roques gives at the end of his treatise on funguses a long list of his mycophilous friends, including in the number many of the most eminent *medical* men of the French capital—if medical men are more careful of what they eat than their neighbours, which, however, is exceedingly doubtful.

† "To eat raw mushrooms" was a proverbial expression among the Greeks, as is shown by the passage which Athenæus quotes out of a play of Antiphanes, called the 'Proverbs':—'Ἐγὼ γὰρ ἂν τῶν ὑμετέρων φάγοιμί τι, μύκητας ὠμοὺς αὐτίκ' ἂν φαγεῖν δοκάω.

St. John when he emerged, after one hour's cooking, from a caldron of boiling oil. In a word, that which has been the daily bread of nations—the poor man's manna—for many centuries, cannot be an unwholesome, much less a dangerous food.* Funguses, no doubt, are a rich and dainty fare; and so whatever objections apply to made-dishes *in genere* may apply also to these, which, while they contain all the sapid and nutritious constituents of animal food, have however an advantage over it—viz. that while they are as rich in gravy as any butcher's meat, their texture is more tender, and their specific gravity less. Touching the general question as to the wholesomeness of made-dishes, it might perhaps be stated as a rule, to which there are many exceptions, that the more we vary and combine food, the better chance there is of our digesting it.† "You must assist nature," Hippocrates says,

---

* Those who themselves know better, smile to read such passages as the following, which is to be found in old Gerard's 'Herbal':—"Galen affirms that they (*i. e.* funguses) are all very cold and moist, and therefore do approach unto a venomous and mothering facultie, and engender a clammy and pituitous nutriment; if eaten, therefore, I give my advice unto those that love such strange and new-fangled meates, to beware of licking honey among thorns, lest the sweetnesse of the one do not counterraille the sharpnesse and pricking of the other."

† A life of labour, no doubt, will make the sorriest fare sit more lightly on the healthy stomach, than the most dainty viands which have been received into an organ that is weakened and goaded by a life of dissipation and excess; but this does not prove sorry fare to be more wholesome than that of a richer kind. No! Dyspepsia is a disease of the rich; not because they live upon the fat of the land, but plainly because they indulge in too large a quantity at a meal. Let the peasant and the lord change places for a week; place the healthy rustic at the rich man's table, and Dives again at the other board, what would be the results to both? Would not the poor man, think you, find indigestion in ragoût, fricassees, truffles, with light wine *ad libitum* to drink with them? and would not the rich man find that the fat pork and hard beer were worse poison than any of the made-dishes, against which he has been so lavish in his blame? In general, no doubt, to be "the happiest of mortals—to digest well" (Voltaire), men should look more to the *quantum* and less to the *quale* of what they eat; but they should pay some attention to this too.

"by art. You must vary your viands and your drinks. Music would tire if it were always to the same tune, so also does a monotonous regimen tire.* Cooks therefore make *mixed* dishes, and he who should always make the same dish would deservedly pass for not being a cook at all."† And though Sydenham, in apparent discordance with this, recommends *one* dish for dinner, it is quite for another reason. Plain food may indeed suit some stomachs, but good cooking suits all stomachs; and when Seneca writes, that "there are as many diseases as cooks," Roques takes him up properly by replying, "Yes; as bad cooks." The rule for every dinner, plain or compound, is to dress it well—"that which is best administered is best;" and good cooking, thus understood as the art of improving and of making the most of a thing, is a matter of equal importance to both rich and poor. It is a safe rule, I believe, and one recommended on good authority too, if men wanted authority on such matter, to eat what they like, but not as much of it as they like.‡ Nine-tenths of

---

* Ἤν δὲ πάντα ὅμοια ποιήσῃ οὐκ ἔχει τέρψιν. Π.Δ. A. 10.

† That I did not always hold such an opinion as the above, to which I have since given in my adhesion, the following ode to Eupepsia, written in the days of theoretical inexperience, will sufficiently testify. I am now convinced that Hippocrates was right!—

Happy the man whose prudent care
  Plain boiled and roast discreetly bound;
Content to feed on homely fare,
  On British ground!
Sound sleep renounces *sugared* peas!—
  No nightmares haunt the modest ration
Of tender steak, that yields with ease
  To mastication!
From stews and steams that round them play,
  How many a tempting dish would floor us,
Had nature made no toll to pay
  At the pylorus!

He dines unscathed, who dines *alone!*
  Or shuns abroad those *corner* dishes;
No Roman garlics make him groan,
  Nor matelotte fishes.
Then let not Vérey's treacherous skill,
  Nor Véfour's, try thy peptic forces;
One comes to swallow many a pill
  Where many a course is!
With *mushroomed* dishes cease to strive;
  Nor for that *truffled crime* inquire,
Which nails the hapless goose alive,
  At Strasburg's fire.

‡ Heberden wisely left it to his patients, except in acute cases of disease or when they were gluttons, "to eat what pleased them, finding that many apparently unfit substances" (*which funguses are not*) "agreed with the

dyspeptics become so from overfeeding. "Nauseosa satietas non ex crassis et pravis solum, sed etiam boni succi alimentis provenit." Even Paracelsus, though an undoubted quack, might give some people a hint: "Dosis sola facit ut venenum sit vel non; cibus enim vel potus qualibet quantitate majore æquo assumtus venenum fit." Dyspeptics are willing to enlist your sympathies in their behalf by telling of the delicacy of their mucous membrane, just as young countesses descant with more success on the extreme susceptibility of their nerves; nor is it always kindly received, if a well-wisher should remind them that their sufferings may not after all have been the fault either of their stomach or of the dish which they blame, but of their own indiscreet use of both. Whilst it is an acknowledged fact on all hands that infants are overfed, and that all children overfeed, men are by no means so prone or willing to admit that gluttony is perhaps the very last of childish things that they are in the habit of putting away from them. Thus, then, though funguses are not to be considered unwholesome, they are, like other good things, to be eaten with discretion and not *à discrétion*. "If you live an indolent life, are a sybarite in your heart, or should some violent passions (choler, jealousy, or revenge) be dealing with you, take care in such a case how you eat ragouts of truffles or of mushrooms; but if, on the contrary, your health be good, your life temperately prudent, your

stomach merely because they were suitable to its feelings." Why quote Abernethy?—but that good sense, backed by personal experience in such matters, are always worth quoting—who says, "Nothing hurts me that I eat with appetite and delight;" or Withers, unless for a like reason, who is "of opinion that the instinct of the palate, not misguided by preconceived opinion, may be satisfied, not only with impunity, but even with advantage." It is the rule by which the brute creation is taught to shun its poison and to choose its food; to a considerable extent, it should be ours also.

temper even, and your mind serene, then (provided you like them) you may eat of these luxuries without the slightest apprehension of their disagreeing with you." M. Roques adds, and with truth, "it is the wine, surcharged with alcohol, of which men drink largely, in order, as they say, to relish and digest their mushrooms and made-dishes, that disagrees with the stomach, and that will, ere long, produce those visceral obstructions, and those nephritic ailments, at once so grievous to bear and so difficult to get rid of."* If the reader shall retain *one* word of the following homely lines, and that word the last, so as to remember it in place, he will owe us no fee, and it will save him many a bitter draught :—

> Lies the last meal all undigested still?
> Does chyle impure your poisoned lacteals fill?
> Does Gastrodynia's tiny gimlet bore,
> Where the crude load obstructs the rigid door?
> Or does the fiery heartburn flay your throat?
> Do darkling specks before your eyeballs float?
> Do fancied sounds invade your startled ear?
> Does the stopt heart oft wake to pulseless fear?
> Your days all listless, and your nights all dream,
> Of Pustule, Ecchymose, and Emphyseme;
> Till ruthless surgeon shall your paunch explore,
> And mark each spot with mischief mottled o'er;
> Does all you suffer quite surpass belief?
> Has oft-tried soda ceased to give relief?
> Has bismuth failed, nor tonics eased your pain?
> Have Chambers, Watson, both been teased in vain?
> In case so cross—what cure?—but one: *Refrain!*

But the objection against funguses is generally of another kind: many persons who like good living too well to be afraid of the new introduction of a luxury which is to bring new dyspepsias for them in consequence, fear lest, whilst indulging in this "celestial manna," this $\beta\rho\hat{\omega}\mu\alpha\ \theta\epsilon\hat{\omega}\nu$, they should

---

* Roques, 'Traité sur les Champignons.'

meet with the fate of the Emperor Claudius, and prefer remaining *vivi* to the chance of becoming *divi* before their time. Now there is really no just ground for this fear; the esculent fungus never becomes poisonous, nor, conversely, the poisonous variety fit to eat. In Claudius's particular case we must remember that Locusta medicated, and Agrippina cooked, that celebrated dish, in which the mushrooms, after all, were but the vehicle for the poison. As to the general fact, though cultivation undoubtedly produces considerable changes in the qualities of this, as in those of other classes of plants, they are never of such a kind as to convert that which is esculent in one locality into a dangerous food in another. "Cœlum non animum mutat;" οὐ γὰρ τὸν τρόπον ἀλλὰ τὸν τόπον μόνον μετήλλαξα.* That the mushroom is not quite so wholesome when cultivated as it is in the meadow,† in a state of nature, cannot be doubted;‡ and that many persons have suffered, both in France and England, more or less gastric disturbance after eating those taken from hotbeds or from dark foul macerated places, is certain; that mushrooms also in decay, when chemistry has laid hold of their tissues and changed their juices, have produced disagreeable sensations in the stomach and bowels, is not to be questioned; finally, that the idiosyncrasy of some persons is opposed to this diet, as that of others is to shell-fish, to melons, cucumbers, and the like, must also be ceded: but none of these admissions surely meddle with the question, nor go any way towards proving the assumed fact, viz. that a mushroom ever changes its nature

* Æschines.
† "Pratensibus optima fungis Natura est."—*Horace.*
‡ Locality has a great effect upon almost all that we eat: our very mutton varies in different counties; compare the town-bred gutter-fed poultry of London with that of twenty miles around; fish vary, the tench out of different ponds are different; fruits vary with the soil; are potatoes everywhere the same?

and becomes poisonous like the toadstool.* It has been unwarily asserted, that because the people of the north are in the habit of employing in their kitchen the *Agaricus muscarius,* which is known to be poisonous in the south, this points to some remarkable difference in the plant depending on difference of locality. It is to be recollected, however, that this very same fungus, if taken in sufficient quantity, without the precaution usually adopted of soaking it in vinegar before cooking, *has* produced fatal accidents, of which we read the recitals in various mycological works; and only not more frequently because the plant, being generally well steeped in brine or acetic acid, is in most cases robbed of deleterious principles, the only residue left being pure fungine, which is equally innoxious and the same in all funguses whatever. It is moreover worthy of remark, that though the common mushroom (*Ag. campestris*) varies considerably both as to flavour and wholesomeness (circumstances attributable in part to the varieties of soil in which it flourishes †), other funguses, on the contrary, being mostly restricted for their alimentation and reproduction to some one particular habitat, do not present such differences. The *Boletus edulis,* the *Fistulina hepatica,* the *Agaricus oreades,* the *Ag. procerus,* the *Ag. prunulus,* the *Ag. fusipes,* the *Cantharellus cibarius,* etc., are, in flavour and other sensible qualities, just the same in England as they are in France, Switzerland, or Italy. Thus the

---

* Persons have fancied themselves poisoned when they were not; indigestion produced by mushrooms is looked upon with fear and suspicion, and if a medical man be called in, the stomach-pump used, and relief obtained, nothing will persuade either patient or practitioner that this has not been a case of poisoning. "You have saved my life," says the one. "I think you will not be persuaded to eat any more mushrooms for some time," says the other: and so they part, each under the impression that he knows more about mushrooms than anybody else can tell him.

† It grows not only throughout Europe, but in India also.

objection to eat funguses on the ground of their presenting differences depending on those of the locality where they grow, applies principally, if it applies at all, to the English mushroom, of which no housekeeper is afraid, and by no means to those species the introduction of which into our markets and kitchens forms the main object of this treatise.

Besides the foregoing objections to funguses on the general ground of their supposed indigestibility, or else the more particular one of their not being at all times and in all places the same, a further and weightier one, as it is commonly urged, is the alleged impossibility of our being able to discriminate, with certainty, the good from the bad; an objection which derives much of its supposed weight from the apparently clashing testimonies of authors respecting the same species, who not unfrequently describe, under a *common* name, a fungus which some of them assert to be esculent, some doubtful, and others altogether poisonous in its qualities. Such discrepancies, however, have already in many cases been satisfactorily adjusted, whilst a more minute attention and corresponding improvement in the pictorial representation of species is daily diminishing the errors of the older mycologists.

Admitting then, what there is no gainsaying, the existence of many dangerous individuals in this family,* ought we not, in a matter of such importance, rather to apply ourselves to the task of discriminating them accurately† than permit idle

---

* We should apply the same rules of discrimination here as elsewhere. Have we not picked potatoes for our table out of the deadly family of *Solana?* selected with care the *garden* from the *fool's* parsley? And do we not pickle gherkins, notwithstanding their affinity to the *Elaterium momordicum*, which would poison us if we were to eat it?

† "N'est-il pas bien plus simple et bien plus sûr en même temps, puisqu'on le peut, de prévenir les maux, que de spéculer sur les moyens si souvent incertains de les guérir?"—Bull. Pl. Vénén. p. 11.

rumours of its impracticability, or even its real difficulty, to dehort us from the undertaking? Assuredly nature, who has given to brutes an instinct, by which to select their aliment, has not left man without a discriminative power to do the same with equal certainty; nor does he use his privileges to their full, or employ his senses as he might, when he suffers himself to be surpassed by brute animals in their diagnosis of food.

MODES OF DISTINGUISHING.

The first thing to know about funguses is, that in the *immense majority of cases* they are harmless; the innoxious and esculent kinds are the *rule*, the poisonous the *exceptions* to it; in a general way, it is more easy to say what we should not eat than what we may; we should never eat any that smell sickly or poisonous. Opinions respecting the agreeableness or disagreeableness of an odour, as of a taste, may differ; thus, in France and Italy (where the palate seems to us to bribe the judgment of the nose), it is usual to speak of that of the *Ag. prunulus* as "perfuming the air;"* but though the strong peculiar smell exhaled by this and some other esculent funguses is anything but a perfume, as we apprehend the term, it is very different from that intolerable fœtor, that nauseous overwhelming odour given out by the *Phallus impudicus*, the *Clathrus cancellatus*, the *Amanita verna*, and its varieties. There are some indeed which, yielding no smell, will poison notwithstanding; but then there are none to lure us into a false security by a deceitful fragrance. The same negative indications are furnished by the palate as by the nose; those that are bitter, or styptic, or that burn the fauces on mastication, or that parch the throat when they have been

* *Vide* Vittadini and Roques.

swallowed, should be put aside; those that yield spiced milk, of whatever colour, should be held, notwithstanding exceptions, in suspicion, as an unsafe dairy to deal with. The "Lucchese Goat" (*Ag. piperatus*) and the "Cow of the Vosges" (*Ag. lactifluus aureus*), though in high request in their respective localities, and really delicate themselves, are akin to others whose milks, though they may have the colour of gold, have the qualities of gamboge.

"———— Nescius auræ
Fallacis,
Qui nunc te fruitur credulus *aurea!*"

Paulet was once so indiscreet as to eat a slice of the Griper (*Ag. torminosus*), which belongs to this genus, and afterwards still more indiscreet in giving it the inviting name of " Mouton zoné;" it is well, however, that the reader should be apprised, as he will frequently come across this 'mouton' in his walks, that it is a perfect wolf in sheep's clothing, nor less to be avoided than one nearly allied to it, which rejoices in the name of *necator*, or the slayer.* Here, as it is a safe rule rather to condemn many that may be innocent than to admit one that is at all suspicious to our confidence, we should, till intimacy has made us familiar with the exceptions, avoid all those the flesh of which is livid, or that, chameleon-like, assume a variety of hues on being broken or bruised.† The

* Roques fell in with two soldiers at St. Cyr, who had gathered and were in the act of carrying off twice the quantity of this fungus necessary to kill the regiment, when he interfered, and no doubt saved many lives in doing so. The soldiers, it appears, had mistaken the *Ag. necator* for the *Hydnum repandum*, to which it bears some slight resemblance in colour, and in nothing else.

† The *converse* of this remark by no means holds true; the *Amanita verna*, the *Am. phalloides*, the *Ag. semiglobatus, dryophilus*, and *muscarius*, though amongst the most deadly of this class of plants, do not change colour on being cut; the flesh of the first two is, moreover, of a tempting whiteness, like that of the common puff-ball, than which there is not a safer or a better fungus. "Omnino ne crede colori" is our only safe motto here.

external colour furnishes no certain information—with the single exception of that of the gills in one or two Agarics—by which to know the good from the bad; thus, the "Boule de Neige" and the Vernal Amanite are both white; but the dress, in one case, is of innocence, in the other of mere hypocrisy; again, the green, which we are so cautioned to avoid in this class of plants as chlorotic and unhealthy, and which is of such bad augury in *Amanita viridis*, is quite the contrary in the *Verdette* (*Ag. virescens*). So that to be led only by colour would certainly be to be misled—a mistake which, in the family of the *Russulæ*, might readily compromise life.

Some mycologists recommend, with certain exceptions, the avoidance of such Agarics as have lateral stalks, of such as are pectinate (*i.e.* have equal gills, like a comb), of such as have little flesh in proportion to the depth of their gills, and generally, of all those that are past their prime. Some warn us not to eat after the snail, as we are in the habit of doing in our gardens after the wasp; we may trust, it seems, to him to point out the best greengages, but not to the slug to select our mushrooms for us. Finally, it has been very currently affirmed, though I think without sufficient warrant, that all such funguses as run rapidly into deliquescence ought to be avoided as dangerous. Here, while it might be unsafe to lay down any positive rule beyond one's own experience, this, so far as it goes, would rather lead me to a different inference; and even the reader will ask—Does not the mushroom deliquesce, and is not ketchup, that "poignant liquor made from boiled mushrooms mixed with salt,"* to which we are all so partial, this very deliquescence? But, besides this, the *Ag. comatus*, which is highly deliquescent, is largely eaten about Lucca; the *Ag. atramentarius* also is, on our own authority,

* Johnson's Dictionary.

periculo ventris nostri, as good for ketchup as for that purpose to which its juices are more commonly put, viz. for making ink. Thus, amongst deliquescent Agarics, **there are** some the **juices of which are** both safe and savoury, perhaps of more than those here recorded; but **as** I have not hitherto myself made trial of any others, and as **there are** some dangerous species mixed up with this group, the public cannot be too much cautioned against making any rash experiment, where the consequences of a mistake might be so serious.

Some trees give origin by preference to good, others to deleterious species; thus, the hazel-nut, the black and perhaps the white poplar, together with the fig-tree, grow only good sorts; whereas the olive has been famous, since the days of Nicander, for none but poisonous species.

> "The rank in smell, and those of livid show,
> All that at roots of oak * or olive grow,
> Touch not! But those upon the fig-tree's rind
> Securely pluck—a safe and savoury kind!"

The elm, the alder, the larch, the beech, and some other trees, seem capable of supporting both good and bad species at their roots; hence it is not safe to trust implicitly to the *tree* to determine the wholesomeness or unwholesomeness of the fungus that grows out of it, or in its neighbourhood. The presence of a *free acid* is by no means conclusive either way, there being many species of both good and bad, which will indifferently turn litmus-paper red. The old and very general practice adopted by cooks of *dressing funguses with a silver spoon* (which is supposed to become tarnished, then, only when their juices are of a deleterious quality), is an error which cannot be too generally known and exposed, as many lives, especially on the Continent,

---

* He was wrong here: the oak produces both the *Fistulina hepatica* and the *Agaricus fusipes*, two excellent funguses, particularly the last, which, properly dressed or pickled, have not many rivals.

have been, and still are, sacrificed to it annually. In some cases the kitchen-fire will extract the deleterious property from the funguses, which it would have been unsafe to eat raw, and frequently the acrid lactescent kinds change their nature entirely and become mild by cooking; in other cases, the virus is drawn out by saturating the fungus, sometimes before dressing it, either in vinegar or brine,* the liquid then containing the poison which was originally in the plant; but in other species, as in *Ag. emeticus*, it would seem from the experiments of M. Krapf, of Vienna, upon living animals, that it is to be extracted neither by ebullition nor desiccation.†

The effects produced by the poison of mushrooms are exceedingly various, that is to say, the virus itself differs in different species, both as to *kind* and, where that is the same, as to the *degree* of its concentration; it is generally, however, of the class called acro-narcotic, producing inflammatory affections of the intestines, and exerting a deleterious influence over the whole nervous system. In cases where only a very small quantity has been taken experimentally, a constriction of the fauces has followed, and continued for a period varying from some minutes to several hours, occasioning, or not, nausea, heat, and, in some instances, even pain of the stomach; "sometimes the affection is entirely confined to the head, and a stupor or light delirium succeeds the eating of some species, and continues for two or three days."‡ Not unfrequently, as in those cases cited by Larber, the symptoms have been altogether those of cholera, without any cerebral disturbance what-

* As was known to the Greeks, 'Prepare your funguses with vinegar, salt, or honey, for thus you will rob them of their poison,' οὕτω γὰρ αὐτῶν τὸ πνιγῶδες ἀφαιρεῖται.

† Vittadini, however, ate largely of this fungus, which he describes as very disagreeable, though it did not prove poisonous to him.

‡ Puccinelli.

ever; but in other instances that have come to my knowledge, during a several years' residence on the Continent, these have been of a mixed character,* in which both the head and viscera have participated; and the autopsies after death have, in accordance with the symptoms, shown the stomach and intestines more or less disorganized with the products of inflammation, together with a congested state of the brain or of its investments, or a local or general softening of its substance.† The poison, as has been said, exists in very different

* In a whole family, cut off in the year 1843, at Lucca, by dining on some poisonous Boletuses, drawn and first described by Professor Puccinelli under the ominous name of *Boletus terribilis*, besides most extensive ulceration of the mucous coat of the intestines throughout a very considerable portion of their extent, together with injection of the vessels of the brain, the lungs were found congested, and the cavities of the heart distended, with coagula of blood.

† For a most interesting record of all the more recent poisonings from funguses in Italy, the reader may consult Professor delle Chiaje's work on Toxicology. The following, the only one I shall give, is to be found in Vittadini's excellent work on funguses:—

"Giovanna Ballerini, montanara, d'anni 26, moglie di Luigi Dodici, nativa di Brugnello, Stato Sardo, e domiciliata in Lardirago, distretto di Belgiojoso, provincia di Pavia, mangiò la sera del 19 maggio, 1831, in compagnia di due suoi nipoti, Giuseppe Ballerini d'anni 6, e Maria, d'anni 12, buona copia d'agarici di primavera, cotti nella minestra. Erano dessi stati colti nel vicin bosco della Rossa, e da quella sventurata probabilmente scambiati coi Prugnuoli (*Ag. mouceron*, Bull.), funghi generalmente conosciuti da quegli alpigiani sotto il nome di Spinaroli, o Maggenghi. All' indomani allontanossi Giovanna da casa, come era suo costume, onde provvedere ai proprj bisogni, ma trascorse alcune ore venne assalita da forte oppressione all' epigastrio, da nausee, da conati di vomito, ecc., e costretta infine verso il meriggio dalla gravezza del patire a tornarsene a casa, ove trovò dallo stesso male tormentati anche i nipoti. I principali fenomeni morbosi che presentavano quegli infelici all' arrivo di Giovanna erano: nausee continue, dolori acutissimi allo stomaco ed alle intestina, deliquj frequenti, convulsioni, ecc. Poco dopo Maria ed in seguito Giovanna vennero prese da vomito ostinato di materie bigio-nerastre, a cui s'accoppiava bentosto, per colmo di sventura, un' abbondante soccorrenza della stessa materia, e più innanzi di pretto sangue. Impotente a recere, Giuseppe si struggeva in vani conati di vomito. Chiamato verso sera in loro soccorso il sig. dott. Luigi Casorati, medico condotto del luogo, mio collega ed

degrees of intensity in different species. In some, as the *Amanita verna*, a few grains of the fresh fungus suffice to kill a dog;* while the *Agaricus muscarius*, though equally fatal in sufficient quantities, is not nearly so strong. Some time in general elapses from the swallowing the poison to that in which its deleterious workings first begin to be felt. I have heard of cases (similar to those cited in the last note) of persons who had supped overnight on the meal that was to prove their last, who have slept, risen next morning, gone to work, and continued working for hours, before they have been made aware of their condition. When, however, the symptoms have once

amico, s' adoperò ma invano per sostare il vomito ed il colera, che specialmente in Maria ed in Giovanna andavano sempre più imperversando. Le bevande mucilaginose, il latte, gli oppiati, le fomentazioni ammollienti sull' addome a nulla giovarono. Si tentò la sanguigna, ma anche questa senza effetto. Alle ore 7 del mattino del giorno 21, 38 ore circa dall' ingestione del fungo, Giuseppe, chi si era ostinatamente rifiutato ad ogni medicina, non era più; nè miglior sorte incontravano Maria e Giovanna, chi, tradotte all' ospedale di Pavia, non ostante i soccorsi che vennero loro prodigati, perivano nella stessa giornata fra le più terribili angosce, e senza perdere gran fatto l' uso dei sensi, la prima verso il meriggio, l' altra verso le ore sette pomeridiane. All' autopsia del cadavere di Giuseppe Ballerini, eseguitasi in Lardirago, sotto i miei occhi, dallo stesso Dottor Casorati che gentilmente me ne fece invito, ed alla quale assisteva pure il sig. dott. G. Galliotti, si trovò lo stomaco zeppo di un liquido verdastro, entro cui nuotavano ancora, unitamente a buona porzione di riso e di erbe, varj pezzetti del fungo non ancora decomposti, e che potei agevolmente riconoscere a qual parte della pianta appartenessero; la mucosa di quel viscere sensibilmente injettata, e coperta, specialmente lungo la piccola curvatura ed in vicinanza del piloro, di grandi macchie di color roseo-livido intenso. Le intestina tenui pur esse ove più ove meno injettate, e del color dello scarlatto, le crasse morbosamente ristrette, ma meno delle tenui ingorgate; sì le une che le altre vuote d'alimenti, e non contenenti che poca quantità di muco bigio-nerastro e qualche lombrico. Le meningi erano anch' esse sommamente injettate, specialmente la pia; la sostanza del cervello meno consistente del naturale, punteggiata di rosso, e la base dello stesso nuotante in una quantità considerabile di siero sanguinolento."—*Vitt.* p. 310.

* When dried, gr. xx.-xxv. will scarcely produce the effects of gr. v. of the fungus when first gathered.—*Vitt.*

set in, they become rapidly more and more alarming, while the chances of arresting or mitigating their excruciating severity lessen every minute. As the evils to be apprehended from the agency of these plants can only be prevented by their instant evacuation, to assist the disposition to vomit, or, if called in early enough, to anticipate it by the milder emetics in sufficient doses (surely not by strong ones, as some have recommended!), and, when the stomach has been thoroughly evacuated, to relieve the violence of the pain by bland mucilaginous drinks, with opiates, are the indications plainly pointed out, and the means by which inflammation and subsequent sphacelus of the gut, as well as the deleterious effects produced on the nervous system by the absorption of the poison into it, have been occasionally averted; but should symptoms of great depression be already present (as too frequently happens before the medical man arrives), he will endeavour, in that case, to rally the vital powers (scanty though the chances of success will then be) by small and repeated doses of sulphuric ether and ammonia combined, or should head symptoms require his interference, he must in that case bleed.

CONDITIONS NECESSARY TO THEIR GROWTH.

Of these, in fact, we know but little, and in the great majority of instances absolutely nothing; in a few cases moisture* and heat seem alone sufficient, even in our own hands, to

* The total quantity of moisture absorbed by fungses, during development and growth, is great; thus, if a number of small Agarics, still in their wrappers, be placed in wineglasses half filled with water, this will be rapidly absorbed, even before they break through their membrane. Moreover, if Agarics or Boletuses, already developed, be placed in glasses containing so many ounces of water, the amount of which has been previously ascertained, and equal to that in another glass, by which to make allowance for what has been lost by evaporation, the result will generally be that a quantity of water, equal to from one-

cause some of them to grow; in others, electricity appears indispensable. A wet autumn is generally found to be exceedingly prolific in these plants, with the following notable difference as to *kind*: all those that are parasitical on trees show themselves, during a wet season, in amount directly varying with that of the previous rain, irrespective of any other influences conspiring to give this effect; whilst those, on the other hand, which issue from the earth, when the surface of this has been long chilled or when the electrical state of the air has not been materially modified for some time, will be found to come up sparingly or not at all, whatever rain may have fallen. An exception to this rule occurs in the common mushroom, which, by the combination of certain degrees of heat and moisture, may be reared throughout the year without the co-operation of electricity. A variety of plans have been recommended for this purpose, many of which are both troublesome and expensive; the following, taken by M. Roques from a scientific work on gardening, and said to be infallible, has, if so, the great advantage of extreme simplicity to recommend it:—" Having observed that all those dunghills which abounded chiefly in sheep- or cow-droppings, began shortly to turn mouldy on their surface and to bear mushrooms, I collected a quantity of this manure, which, so soon as it began to turn white, I strewed lightly over some melon-beds and some spring crops of vegetables, and obtained in either case, and as often as I repeated the experiment, a ready supply of excellent mush-

fourth to one-third of the full weight of each fungus, will have been absorbed and exhaled again in two days. The redundant moisture of these plants is rendered conspicuous if we place a Boletus on a watch-glass, the surface of which is speedily beaded with drops of water, as if it had been in the rain; while the quantity of fluid is sometimes so great as to defeat the object we had in placing it there, viz. that of collecting the spores.

rooms, which came up from a month to six weeks after the dung had been so disposed of; but as an equable temperature is in all cases desirable to render the result certain, where this cannot be secured under the protection of glass, the next best plan is to scatter a portion of the above dungs mixed with a little earth in a cave or cellar, to which some tan is an excellent addition; for tan, though it kills other vegetable growths, has quite an opposite effect on funguses."

Next to the common mushroom, in regard to the success attending its cultivation, comes that of the *Pietra funghaia*, a plant unknown to Clusius, but described by Mathiolus and Imperato, under the name of the 'stony fungus.' Cesalpinus has added to their accounts, directions for procuring it the whole year through, which, he says, is to be done either by irrigating the soil over the site of the stone, or by transferring the *Pietra funghaia* with a portion of the original mould, and watering it in our own garden. Porta adds, that the funguses take seven days to come to perfection, and may be gathered from the naked block (where this has been properly moistened) six times a year; but in preference to merely watering the blocks, he recommends that a light covering of garden mould should be first thrown over them. The *Pietra funghaia*, though its range of territory be extremely small, lies embedded in a variety of soils, in consequence of which its Polyporus, like our own mushroom, is very various in flavour, depending on the kind of *humus* in which its matrix happens to be placed. Those that grow on the high grounds above Sorrento, and on the sides of Vesuvius, are in less esteem than such as are brought into the Naples market from the mountains of Apulia.*

---

* The reader desirous of a detailed account of this interesting fungus, should consult a small quarto *brochure* published some years ago, by Pro-

A third fungus, which we have the means of producing *ad libitum*, is that which sprouts from the pollard head of the black poplar;* these heads it is usual to remove at the latter end of autumn, as soon as the vintage is over, and their marriage with the vine is annulled; hundreds of such heads are then cut and transported to different parts; they are abundantly watered during the first month, and in a short time produce that truly delicious fungus, *Agaricus caudicinus*, the *Pioppini*, which, during the autumn of the year, make the greatest show in many of the Italian market-places. These pollard blocks continue to bear, for from twelve to fourteen years; I saw a row of them in the botanic garden at Naples, which, after this period, were still productive, though less frequently, and of fewer Agarics at a crop. The practice of rearing funguses from the poplar is not modern; Dioscorides knew, for he tells us that if we "bark the white or black poplar, cutting the bark into pieces and covering it with horse-dung, an excellent kind of fungus will spring up, and continue to bear throughout the year:" by way of comment to which passage Mathiolus adds, that a little leaven † will produce an abundant crop in four days. Another fungus, which I have myself reared (*Polyporus avellanus*), is to be procured by singeing over a handful of straw a block of the cob-nut tree, which is then to be watered and put by. In about a month the funguses make their appearance, which are quite white, of from two to three inches in diameter, and

fessor Gasparini, of Naples, who was preparing a second edition in the autumn of 1844, with numerous additions, which has, no doubt, been reprinted.

* Or rather, as Professor Tenore has told me, from the *Populus nigra*, var. *Neapolitana*.

† Müller declares that fermentation is itself a fungus, which continues to feed and multiply so long as it finds the elements of nutrition in the liquid in which it originates. This, then, is employing one fungus life to evoke another.

excellent to eat; while their profusion is sometimes so great, as entirely to hide the wood from which they spring.* Dr. Thore says, that in the Landes, the *Boletus edulis* and *Ag. procerus* are constantly raised by the inhabitants of that district, from a watery infusion of the said plants; that something more than this, however, is necessary, seems certain, since during the two or three years during which I frequented the baths of Lucca, and was in the habit of using infusions of these and a variety of other funguses, often throwing them over the very spots where each kind grew, my experiments never succeeded. Nor was Pr. Puccinelli, of Lucca, who repeated similar experiments in the botanic garden there, much more successful. Briganti, of Naples, told me much the same story; and Sanguinetti at Rome was equally unsuccessful with Ottaviani at Urbino. On making inquiry of friends in England who have attempted to propagate different kinds of funguses, either by infusion or otherwise, their attempts generally failed. My friend Mrs. Hussey, in particular, acquaints me that she has been in the habit of subjecting many plants to a like experiment, and with similar want of result. Lastly, as concerning truffles, Mr. Bornholtz has given directions how to rear them, which, as they are exceedingly expensive and troublesome, must needs be infallible to secure proselytes, even among the most sworn amateurs of these delicacies. "Prepare your ground," says he, "with oak leaves in decay; you must also mix some iron with it and take care to make it of a proper consistence, either

---

* All blocks of this nut-wood do not bear. Professor Sanguinetti informs me that the peasants in the Abruzzi, who bring in these logs, know perfectly which will succeed and which will not; "a knowledge," he adds, "to which closest attention during all the years that I have been employed by the Papal Government as superintendent of the fungus market, has not yet enabled me to attain."

by adding sand, should it be too compact, or clay, should it be of too light a nature; having then with great care transplanted your truffles, (which must be properly packed with a quantity of the original mould about them,) they are to be placed tenderly in the new settlement, covered over lightly with mould, and this again is to be covered with boughs of oak and *Carpinus Betulus* to protect the deposit from molestation; neither must you consider your work completed till a sacred grove of these particular trees has been planted round it, which must be done with such precaution, that while they keep the precious ground in a perpetual twilight, they must not obstruct it too much, but leave a certain free passage to the air." After which injunctions, if they be carefully attended to, Mr. B. assures us that we can reckon, without fear of disappointment, on a dish of truffles, whenever we may want them for ourselves or our friends.

FAIRY RINGS.

We know as little of the origin of fairy-rings, as of any other phenomenon connected with the growth of funguses. These fairy-rings are of all sizes, from one and a half to thirty feet in diameter; the grass composing them is observed in spring, to be of a thicker growth than the surrounding herbage, and, in consequence of the manure afforded by the crop of last year, is of a darker colour. Within these rings are frequently seen certain varieties of this class of plants, very generally Agarics, though puff-balls frequently, and occasionally the *Boletus subtomentosus*, affect a similar mode of growth. Of the Agarics which appear in these circles, some of the principal are *Agaricus oreades*, *Ag. prunulus*, *Ag. Orcella*, *Ag. Georgii*, *Ag. personatus*, and *Ag. campestris*. As all these feed at the expense of the grass, (by exhausting the ground that would otherwise have furnished it with the necessary supplies,) the richest vegetation in the field is generally the first to become seared. These rings (giving birth to some one species which, dying, is not unfrequently succeeded by another a little later, and this perhaps by a third, in the same order of occurrence) continue to enlarge their boundaries for a long but indefinite period.

It seems not easy to determine precisely, to the operation of what cause or causes the increase in the size of these circles from year to year should be attributed. Is it the projectile force with which the spores are disseminated all round, that has carried them so uniformly beyond the margin of the last ring as to form a concentric circle for the next of larger diameter beyond? Or is the cause to be sought underground, in the general spread of the spawn of last year in all directions outwards, but only fertile in a concentric ring *beyond* the site of the last crop, which had already exhausted the ground, and so rendered it incapable of supporting any new vegetable life? Or do both these causes conspire in this result? The quantity of spawn and of the spores necessarily contained in it, and the depth to which they penetrate under the surface of the soil, renders the possibility of their spreading in the latter way easily conceivable.*

ON THE DEVELOPMENT OF FUNGUSES.

"Ins Innre der Natur dringt kein erschaffner **Geist**,
Zu glücklich wem sie nur die äussre Schale lösst."—*Haller.*

It would be an insult to the reader's understanding, and a most idle waste of his time, to attempt to confute such self-

* On digging up the earth in the neighbourhood of a ring in which *A. prunulus* was at the time growing, I found the mould to the depth of a foot

destroying dogmas as those of "spontaneous" or of "equivocal" generation, which last is only a clumsy *équivoque* expressive of the same thing: we might just as well talk of the pendulum of a clock generating the time and space in which it librated, as of dead matter spontaneously quickening and actuating those new movements of which some of its particles have become the seat; for how, in the name of common sense, can that which we assume to be dead, *i.e.* emphatically and totally without life, convey such purely vital phenomena as those of intus-susception and growth, which by the very supposition are no longer within itself? Life, on such an hypothesis as this, ceases to be the opposite and antagonist principle to death, of which it then becomes but a different mode and a new phasis. It is not the incomprehensibility of such a notion (be it well understood) against which the objection lies, for as life begins and ends in mystery, that would be no objection; it lies in the rashness of attempting to solve an admitted mystery, by placing a palpable absurdity in its room; vainly and irreverently arrogating to itself the honours of a discovery which we are to believe if we can! At this rate, addled eggs, abandoned by the vital principle, might take to hatching themselves! A more legitimate and very interesting subject for inquiry is, whether those funguses which are parasitical (*i.e.* derive their support from the structures whence they emanate) are so many separate constituents of a superior life *under analysis*, or each of itself a new individual? In support of the first view, it is urged that since reproduction in such lower existences is nothing but a modification of nutri-

and more, hoary, with an arachnoid spawn strongly charged with the odour of this mushroom. Persoon found that to destroy a fairy-ring of the same Agaric, it was necessary to dig to a considerable depth, when the next crop that came up was disseminated sporadically over the ground.

tion, a new process might well originate from its perversion, and thus give rise to new products; and just as the change in the ordinary nutrition of our bodily organs is prone to give birth to various local disorganizations or morbid growths, such, it is argued, might be the origin of fungoid growth on trees. But then comes the difficulty: such a view does not, and plainly cannot, explain the development of the *not* parasitical kinds, of which the origin should be the same; no, nor even of all that live by suction at the expense of other plants, since there are as many kinds which quicken in *dead* and decaying structures, as there are that issue out of decrepit and *living* ones; here, then, it is plain that perverted nutrition can have nothing to do with their production, for in this case nutrition has, by the supposition, ceased; and to talk of disease *after* death would be a strange figure of speech indeed! An elm or oak is frequently dead five, seldom less than three, years before these parasitical growths make their appearance, from which it would appear to follow that seeds are not developed by, but that they must be extraneous to, and independent of, any pathological relation of the plant from which they grow. If then fungus life be not to be sought for, and cannot with propriety be said to originate in any morbid conditions of the tissues from which they spring, whence do they derive life—in other words, whence in every instance comes that particular seed which, when quickened, is to produce after its kind? Lies this dormant for a season in those dead and decaying tissues, which a little later the plant originating from it is destined to embellish; or is the living germ first brought to them by the winds, and merely deposited on their surface, as in a fitting *nidus* on which their future development is to be effected? Some writers take one view, some another. Many believe the seeds of funguses to come directly from the earth,* and to be drawn up with the sap, which, as it penetrates throughout the tissues of the plant, must carry the seeds also along with it. That such is actually sometimes the case is certain, since we can not only plant parasitical blights of a particular kind so as to infect particular plants, but may also by digging a trench between those that have already become diseased, and those that are still healthy, stay the progress of the blight—thus clearly establishing not only the fact of seeds, but also the highly interesting additional one, of their ascent into the structures of plants by intussusception; and to arrive at a general view from these particular cases, this would seem to be the usual mode of their propagation. Neither does it make against this view nor is it more in favour of the other, which supposes the germs to be derived primarily from the air, and to be thence precipitated on the structures where they grow, that funguses are found on organizations in decay, on withered boughs, and on seared leaves, out of which all sap must of course have been long ago exsiccated; for what then? though the sap does, the seeds do not, evaporate with it. These, once absorbed and diffused during the lifetime of the plant throughout its whole economy, remain there in a state of potential activity, ready to burst forth and germinate whenever the necessary conditions for these wonderful changes shall be presented to them, just as though the seeds of corn now flourishing in different parts of England, had first existed for some thousand years as mummy wheat, potentially and unquickened. Nothing perishes in nature: "destructio unius matrix alterius;" life may change titles, but never becomes extinct; so soon as the more perfect plant dies, a host of other vegetable existences, hitherto en-

* This was the opinion of the Greeks, who called funguses γηγενεῖs, or earthborn.

thralled by laws of an organization superior to their own, now that the connection has been dissevered, put forth their separate energies, and severally assert their independence. The poplar may have perished, root, stem, and branch, but its extinction is only the signal for other existences, which had been heretofore bound up and hid within its own, to assert themselves; and accordingly a Polyporus sprouts out here; here a Thelephora embellishes the dead bark; and here an Agaric springs out of the decaying fibres of its head: these in turn also decay, but as they *moulder* away they languish into a new kind of fungous life, of an inferior type to the last, as if their own vitality were inferior in kind to that of the decayed poplar, whence they lately issued.* Thus, since the seeds of funguses actually exist in great quantity in other plants, and since they occur in the closed interior of fruits and in corollas which are still in their envelopes (in either case out of the reach of the external air); since finally, the *Pietra funghaia*, which produces a Polyporus unknown to England, may be, notwithstanding, made to germinate in England by furnishing the stone with adequate supplies of water and of heat, *that* seems the more tenable hypothesis of the two, which, in every case, supposes the *nidus* of the fungus to furnish the seed, and the atmosphere, the conditions necessary for its quickening. How the seed is first made to quicken is another and most interesting question, still evolved in mystery. As there is no ocular evidence to be obtained of the usual organs of sex,

---

* Just as in the inorganic world, chemical analysis is frequently the precursor of new forms of matter resulting from the new affinities which take place, so when a vegetable dies, and the synthesis of its structural arrangement is broken up, nature frequently avails herself of this season of decomposition, to bring new individuals out of the decaying structures of the old, which, in consequence of a beautiful pre-arrangement, find there all the requisite supplies for their growth and future maintenance.

some mycologists have separated funguses from the family of the clandestinely married *Cryptogamia*, to place them with the *Agamia*, which repudiate the marriage tie;* but as every argument from ignorance is unsafe, (and such would appear to be particularly the case here, when we consider how many things undoubtedly exist, which the imperfection of lenses and the circumscribed power of the eye prevent our seeing,) we should rather make use of what is displayed to us in the economy of other plants, in the way of analogy as applied to these, than deny what is likely, merely because it is not an object of sense. It would appear then, from what has been stated, that certain funguses are produced like other plants, from seeds; and more likely at least, in the parasitic kinds, that such seeds are derived by the plant which supports them from the ground, than deposited from the atmosphere. Before we proceed to the description of species, a few more words remain to be said about these spores, and a brief notice to be taken of those parts that are essential to all, and more especially of such as are characteristic of those higher forms of funguses which are the more immediate subject of the present work.

SPORES OR SEEDS.

All funguses have not seeds,—at least, seeds apparent to us;† but if we reflect that these, even where visible, can do no more than present to our senses the visible tabernacle of that life

---

* Some mycologists however, as Persoon and Roques, conceive that the common dust of puff-balls is analogous to the pollen of the higher plants, while the real seed is to be sought and found in a finer dust, which is entangled in the reticular meshes at the base of these plants. Others suppose the fluid which bathes the interiors of those little organs, in which the seeds are packed, to be in other funguses the source of their fecundation. But these at present are mere conjectures.

† Several byssoid growths are in this predicament.

which is still invisible, and which, not being material, must ever elude our search,* then it will not appear so difficult to conceive that the apparently seedless threads of some particular moulds should include, in their interior, vital germs of some sort, which, being homogeneous with, or of the same colour as, the parenchyma of the mould itself, are invisible— just as we know them to be for a season in puff-balls, in the veins of truffles, or in the *Ayyrium*, the receptacle of which last breaks up, when ripe, into sporidia, which then and not till then become manifest. The seeds of funguses are called spores: in the great majority of cases, the microscope, which brings their shapes under observation (for to the naked eye they appear as dust), presents them to us as round, oval, oblong, or even angular corpuscules, and, more rarely still, echinulate or with a tail. They are as various in size as in shape, the first bearing no proportion whatever to the dimensions of the future plant. They vary, too, greatly in colour, being sometimes of a pure white, and continuing so throughout the whole of their seminal existence; at other times, the white acquires a yellow tinge on drying. Some are brown, some yellow, some pink, some purple, some purple-black, and some pass successively from pink to purple, and from purple to purple-black.† These seeds or spores are sometimes naked, but are much more commonly shut up in little pouches or receptacles, either of a regular or of an irregular shape; the first are called *thecæ*, the latter *sporanges;* thecæ (which are in shape similar to the cases of the same name that used to receive the ancient εἰλίγματα, or scrolls) are small, cylindrical

---

* "Who seek for life in creatures they dissect,
   Will lose it in the moment they detect."— *Pope.*

† The colours of the spores are of considerable practical use in distinguishing the members of the large family of Agarics, some of which are determined by them.

bodies, in which the seeds lie *one over the other, as in a rouleau;* they are themselves let into a *receptacle* (or that part of the fungus the office of which is to receive and support the reproductive organs) in a regular and symmetrical manner, and at length occupy it completely. Not all are prolific; for some, pressing upon others, cause them to abort, leaving wherever this happens, sterile theere, or *paraphyses,* between those that are fertile. *Sporanges* are little globose or turbinated receptacles, frequently furnished with a pedicle, in which the seeds lie without order, as they are themselves inserted symmetrically, or without order, into the receptacle. Sometimes these seeds are packed in series of fours, as in the fimetary Agarics; in other genera, as in the Helvellæ and Morels, they are stored away in series of eights. The spores, so soon as they are ripe, either drop out of the sporiferous membrane (*hymenium*), or, as more frequently happens, are projected from it with an elastic jerk, or else, as is the case of Agarics of a deliquescent kind, return to the earth mixed up with the black liquid into which these ultimately resolve themselves. Sometimes the *whole* external surface of the fungus is dusted with seed; but much more frequently they are restricted to some particular part, and either lie on the upper side, as in the *Pezizæ,* or on that which is beneath, as in the mushroom. The spores generally lie on the outside of the fungus, but in the puff-ball, as every one knows, they are internal, and in such prodigious quantity as sometimes entirely to fill its cavity. It is a speculation from Germany, that spores are capable of altering their forms, and that according to the accidents of climate or soil, they assume this or that type, and give rise at different times to different kinds of funguses; on which it is sufficient to remark, that while there is not the least foundation for such an hypothesis, there is in fact much evidence against it; nature acts by immutable laws and has no changelings. To appeal to experience, when did mushrooms ever spawn toadstools? When was the *Pietra funghaia* ever seen to bring forth anything but its own Polyporus? or the fig, the poplar, or the hazel (when singed and watered to render them prolific) exhibit any but their own particular mushroom? Spores are endowed, like other seeds, with an extraordinary vitality, which may lie dormant in them for an indefinite period; but unlike most other seeds, they seem capable of resisting the prolonged heat of boiling water, infused in which, and poured upon the ground, they are still capable of producing each after its kind. The specific gravity of spores is greater than that of water, as may be seen by placing a mushroom over a glass which contains it, when, falling upon the surface, they presently subside to the bottom. These spores sometimes merely multiply without any further progress in development; sometimes they proceed a certain way only, and then, the conditions necessary for their further advance failing, this is arrested; sometimes, as in the *Sistotrema*, the plant *appears twice* under a *perfect* form, being for part of its existence a *Hydnum*, and during the other half a *Boletus*; but, generally speaking, these minute corpuscular bodies are destined to receive an infinite variety of protean and imperfect forms, and to pass stage by stage, and step by step, to the full attainment of that ultimate one which they assume when their growth has reached its natural limits. Sometimes the spore expands outright into a puff-ball; sometimes it shoots up straight into a club, as in some of the Clavarias; or lies like a bowl, resupinate on the ground and stalkless, as in the *Peziza*; in other cases, it assumes the more perfect but much less simple forms of *Chanterelle, Boletus, Dædalea, Morel*, or *Mushroom*.

DEVELOPMENT OF SEEDS.

The mode in which the organs immediately containing the seeds are formed, differs according to the family. In the tribe of puff-balls, where the seed is formed in the interior of the fungus, there is no hymenium; a few of the internal cells (when the Lycoperdon has attained its full size) begin to enlarge, and these in a short time are found to contain small granules, generally of a determinate number, and moistened by a fluid secreted from within the walls. In such funguses as have an hymenium it is only some of the superficial cells, and these in a particular position in reference to the receptacle, that contain seeds; though perfect identity of structure throughout, is evinced in a conclusive manner if we invert the head of a young fungus on its stalk; for then these thecæ begin to form and to fill themselves with seed, not on the side where they were about to do so previous to this inversion of the head, but on that which was the uppermost and sterile surface, and which, now that it is the undermost, has become prolific. The expansion of a fungus, according to Vittadini, is effected as follows:—"These thecæ," of which we have been speaking, "as they swell, become distended with the contained seed, and mostly so at their free extremity, since they have more room for expansion in that direction than at the other, which is impacted into the substance of the pileus; in consequence of this, a series of wedges are formed which, as the seed continues to distend them, force out the pileus, loosen its marginal connections with the stalk, uncurl its involuted borders, and finally open up its cells, pores, and sinuses."*

* It appears too mechanical an explanation of a phenomenon so purely vital as growth, to make it in any way dependent on a system of wedges, however ingeniously applied.

In those subterranean funguses which mature their seeds below the surface of the ground, the lower portion, so soon as this is accomplished in the upper, suddenly takes to grow upwards, carrying along with it the bag, which, on reaching the surface of the ground, bursts its envelopes and scatters its prolific dust to the winds. All funguses, as has already been observed, have in all probability spores, though in a few instances, of byssoid growths, (Hyphas, Himantias, and Æthelias,) these are not apparent; in most cases too, they are attached to an hymenium, into which, or on the surface of which, they are placed till ripe. One very large tribe, by far the largest, are called *Hymenomycetes*, from ὑμήν, a membrane, and μύκος, a fungus; *i.e.* funguses with a seed membrane: to distinguish them from those other kinds, very small numerically in proportion to themselves, *Gasteromycetes*, in which the seeds, arranged and stored away in particular receptacles, named sporanges or thecæ, are with them included in the belly (γαστήρ) of the fungus, as is the case in truffles and puff-balls. The hymenium, like that curiously doubled-down sheet of paper which conjurors turn into so many shapes, assumes a great variety of forms; running down the gills of the mushrooms and the plaits of the *Cantharellus*, up into the tubes of the Boletuses; sheathing the vegetable teeth of *Hydna*, forming an intricate labyrinth of anastomosing plates in *Dædalea*; now rising into little rough eminences on the surface of the *Thelephoræ*, and now affording a smooth investment to that of the *Clavariæ*. It is covered with a veil, which disappears so soon as the spores begin to ripen, and its protection is no longer required; seen under the microscope, it appears to be wholly made up of thecæ.

SUCCESSIVE DEVELOPMENT OF THE SPORES.

When the spore is to cease to be a spore, and to become a mushroom, the first thing it does is to send forth certain cotton-like filaments, whose interlacings entangle it completely while they also serve to attach it to the place of its birth; these threads (like the spongioles attached to the roots of phænogamous plants, whose name sufficiently explains their office) absorb and bring nourishment to the quickened spore, which then maintains itself entirely by intus-susception. All this takes place before the germ has burst, or the embryo fungus begun to develope its organs. In some instances, these elementary threads are, like the ordinary roots of plants, spread out to a considerable distance underground, forming here and there in their course small bulbs or tubercles, each of which, in turn, becomes a new individual; in others, and more commonly, these spores are sprinkled about unconnectedly, as in the *Pietra funghaia*, affecting certain spots only, which become so many small matrices whereof each furnishes a crop. The union of many germinating granules together with their connecting threads, constitutes mushroom spawn, or, as it is technically called, *carcytes*.* Examined a short time after quickening, the spore is found to have swelled out into a fleshy kernel; which in puff-balls, truffles, and the uterine subterranean families generally, constitutes of itself the whole fungus; this only grows in size afterwards, the substance and original form remaining the same through the entire period of development. In those destined to live under the influence of air and light, this same rudimental nucleus gradually evolves *new parts*, and assumes, as we have seen, a

* "The facility with which these floccose threads are injured, and their connection destroyed, explains," says Vittadini, "the difficulty of transplanting funguses with success."

vast variety of forms, (whereof each particular one is predetermined by the original bias imprinted upon every spore at its creation,) and here there is a manifest analogy with the progressive development of new parts in the higher plants. In such funguses as are wrapped up in a volva or bag, during the earliest period of growth, this furnishes them not only with the means of protection, but of nourishment also. This volva, which is formed by the mere swelling out of the original fleshy bulb, when it has grown to a certain size, exhibits towards its centre the rudiments of the young fungus; of which the receptacle appears first, and all the other parts in succession. The embryo, next taking to grow, in its turn approaches the circumference of the volva, which, having by this time ceased to expand, is burst open, and sometimes with much violence, by the emerging Amanite. As soon as the hymenium has parted with its seed, which falls from it in the form of fine dust, the fungus, collapsing, either withers on its stem, or else dissolves into a black liquid and so escapes to the earth. In such funguses as have not a volva, the basilar or primary nucleus shoots up at once in the form of a cone, and a little later presents at its apex the rudiments of a receptacle or head; by degrees, and frequently by slow degrees,* the perfected structures of the plant are elaborated and spread themselves out into some of the forms mentioned above, of which the clavate is the most simple, and that with gills the most complex. The primary nucleus is formed out of simple cellular membrane, the cells of which, at first elongating, and at length uniting

---

* The great rapidity with which these wonderful changes succeed each other in funguses with a volva, is widely different from what occurs in those that have none. Thus the Morel takes thirty-one days, Geasters six, and many Tubers twelve months for their full development: so that "To come up like a mushroom" is a proverb with limitations.

into little bundles, assume a fibrous appearance; sometimes these fascicular bodies effuse themselves unchanged into the substance of the receptacle, in which they spread out and are lost; at others, a transverse line makes the demarcation between the pileus and stem.* The last part formed in a fungus, generally, is that which bears the seed; and whenever an exception to this occurs, and the seed is formed at an earlier period than usual, nature has in this case provided three membranes, to cover and protect these delicate organs till the plant shall have attained maturity: these are the ring (*annulus*), the veil (*velum*), and the wrapper (*volva*).

OF THE ANNULUS, THE VELUM, AND THE VOLVA.

Of these involucra the first two are partial, the other universal. The Volva is a thick membranaceous covering, originating at the base of the fungus, which it thus connects with the earth, and furnishes, during its fœtal life, with the means of support and nourishment. When this has ceased, and the plant has quitted its wrapper, if this still adhere to the base of the stalk, it is styled manifest (*manifesta*), but if there be no traces of it left, obliterated (*obliterata*). It is *free* when it can be easily detached, and *congenital* when it cannot without laceration. In funguses with bulbous roots it is congenital, in those without bulbs it is free. All funguses that have a volva are of course *volvati*, but as this organ exists in many only so long as they are underground, mycologists are agreed to restrict the term to such alone as retain it afterwards.

* When the base is formed before the receptacle, the fibres are continuous; but when the receptacle has been formed first, as the fibres of the last cannot be transmitted through those already formed, these two parts remain distinct.

The Ring.—This, which differs considerably in form, substance, and in its attachments, is composed either of a continuous sheet of membrane or else of a number of delicately-spun threads, resembling a spider's web,* which in either case passing from the margin of the pileus to the corresponding upper portion of the stem, give way as the plant expands, and either festoon for a season the margin of the cap, or encircle the stalk with a ring. The marginal remains of the Annulus are extremely fugacious, but the ring round the stalk, though generally transitory, is sometimes persistent; it is *superior* or *descending* when originating from the summit of the stem, it descends outwards and downwards to form connections with the rim of the pileus; *inferior* or *ascending* when, coming off from that portion of the stalk which is below the pileus, it ascends to attach itself to this. In a few cases the ring is partly membranaceous and partly composed of radiating arachnoid threads.

The Veil.—Some funguses not only present the ring just mentioned, their hymenium or seed membrane being further protected from harm by a second investment, the veil, *Velum*, the stalk origin of which, when existing in conjunction with an annulus, is below it, but when the fungus is not annulate, the velum rises higher up on the stalk, stretches across to meet and is afterwards reflected over the whole surface of the pileus; on the expansion of the Agaric this investment is entirely broken up, and exhibits those well-known flocks, which have been called by the learned *verrucæ*, but which, as they are generally of a dirty leprous hue, and affect more or less of a circular arrangement, have procured for this whole tribe of Amanites in Italy the uncomely epithet of *tignosi*, or

---

* In the first instance the fungus is called *annulate*, in the second *cortinate*.

scald-heads. Where there has been both a volva and a velum, as sometimes happens in the same fungus, these verrucæ are of different colours according as they are remnants of the first merely, or of both together.* The velum in the sub-genus *Limacium* is a slimy coating adhering to the head of the fungus, which then looks as if it had been dipped in gum mucilage; this generally disappears after a time, leaving the epidermis dry, though sometimes, like the solid membranaceous veil, it is more or less persistent. The waxy covering on the pileus of the *Ag. virescens*, which after a time cracks and tessellates its surface, is only an exudation limited to the upper portion of the cap, and not a veil.

The Stalk.—This, which is absent in many parasitical funguses of the Order *Pileati*, when present, either effuses itself uninterruptedly into the substance of the pileus, which it then, in fact, *forms*, or else supports merely as on a pillar, a distinct line of demarcation showing where the fibres terminate. It assumes a great variety of forms, which serve in many instances to characterize species; besides which peculiarities there are others to be noted, as the mode of its insertion into the pileus, its having or not having a ring, the circumstance of its being scabrous, glossy, or tomentose, reticulated, spotted, or striped, of one colour above and another below, or of its changing colour when bruised, any of which may sometimes assist our diagnosis.

The Pileus.—By far the larger number of funguses mentioned in this work have a pileus, or cap; all such belong to the first great tribe *Pileati*; they include the genera *Agaricus, Boletus, Cantharellus, Morchella, Hydnum, Fistulina,* and

* *i. e.* when these happen to be of different hues originally, the fragments of the veil being in some places covered by those of the wrapper, in others naked.

Polyporus, each of which furnishes its quota of alimentary species, together with many others not esculent. The form of the pileus, like that of the stalk, is various in these different genera, besides being variable in the different species of the same genus; generally it assumes an orbicular or umbrella shape, especially in such funguses as grow solitary on the ground, whilst in others, parasitical on trees, (particularly when they have no stalk,) it is more or less of a half-hemisphere.

The Gills.—Those vertical plates on the under surface of the mushroom, which radiate from the centre to the circumference, like the spokes of a wheel, are called Gills (*lamellæ*); they are not formed, as some have supposed, of layers of the reduplicated seed-membrane alone, but by a prolongation of the fibres of the pileus, which these merely invest. The fibrous structure is most apparent in Agarics with thick gills; in those where the flesh changes colour when bruised; or where, the interposed flesh remaining white, the hymenium is tinged with the colour of the ripening spores. In those funguses which have little flesh the upper surface of the pileus, especially towards the circumference, is frequently furrowed with transverse sulci; these are occasioned by the sinking in of the epidermis along with the fibres of the flesh between the layers of the hymenium, and consequently their position always corresponds precisely to that occupied by the backs of the gills. The end nearest the stalk is termed posterior (*postica*), the opposite extremity anterior (*antica*); the terminations of the lesser gills take place at various distances short of the stalk, which the perfect gills reach, and down which they sometimes course or are decurrent (*decurrentes*); they are said to be adnate (*adnatæ*) when connected at their posterior end; free (*liberæ*) when they do not adhere; remote (*remotæ*) when they terminate at a certain distance from the stem; emarginate (*emarginatæ*) when they are obtusely notched or hollowed out posteriorly; denticulate (*denticulatæ*) when connected by means of a tooth; equal (*æquales*) when all of the same length; forked (*furcatæ*) and branched (*ramosæ*) when they divide in their course, once, or more frequently, or are connected at the sides with the imperfect gills; dedalean (*dædaleæ*) when they anastomose irregularly together; simple (*simplices*) when they are free from all connections; distant (*distantes*) when they are few and wide apart; close (*confertæ*) when they are very numerous and touch each other; serrated (*serratæ*) when notched like a saw; waved (*undulatæ*) when the margin is undulating; and imbricating (*imbricatæ*) when they lie one over another, like tiles.

The Tubes.—Funguses of the genus *Boletus*, etc., present on their under surface, in place of gills, series of small hollow cylinders or tubes; which are for the most part soldered side to side like the cells of a honeycomb, but in the *Fistulina* are unconnected. Like the gills, they are prolongations of the fibres of the pileus, but lined, instead of coated, by the hymenium; their free extremities are the pores, which at first are closed, but afterwards open to let the seed escape: they are generally of equal length and simple, but sometimes in the interior of a large one smaller tubes may be discerned, in which case the first is termed compound. With reference to the stalk, they are either adnate or decurrent, they first appear as a network formed by slight prominences of the fibres of the pileus; if at this early period a portion be removed together with a piece of the flesh, it is reproduced in a few days and the tubes developed as usual. The beautiful reticulations observed on the stalk of some Boletuses are produced by abortive tubes decurrent along their surface.

The Plaits: Venæ, Plicæ.—The plaits of the Chanterelle

are formed like the gills and tubes of the mushroom and Boletus, *i. e.* by the fibres of the flesh running down from the pileus, and invested in a reduplication of the hymenium; with this difference, however, that while in the two latter the seed membrane is divided into as many portions as there are gills or tubes, in the former the continuity of its surface is perfectly unbroken. These plaits (*plicæ*) are always late in appearing, and sometimes are only developed when the fungus is about to cast its seed.

The Spines: Aculei, etc.—The under surface of the pileus in the genus *Hydnum* is shagged with vegetable spines or teeth (*dentes, aculei*) of unequal lengths, generally isolated, but sometimes connected at the base, and formed originally out of a congeries of minute papillæ invested by the hymenium, which gradually elongate their fibres and assume this form. Light seems essential to their production, for if a Hydnum grow in the dark, the teeth shrink up into long threads and are sterile.

METHODICAL DISTRIBUTION

OF THE

BRITISH ESCULENT FUNGUSES.

The primary division of Funguses into *Hymenomycetes* and *Gasteromycetes* is founded upon the position of their seed, which lies, as we have seen, externally in the first, and internally in the members of the second. The funguses described in the present work belong chiefly to the first division, *Hymenomycetes*; to Tribe 1, *Pileati*; and many of them to Genus 1, *Agaricus*. This genus includes a great variety of species, and is distinguished from all other genera by having a fleshy pileus furnished underneath with *gills*, which are placed at right angles to the stem. Some species, during their infancy, are enclosed either in one or more membranes.

Division I. HYMENOMYCETES.
Tribe 1. *PILEATI.*
Genus 1. AGARICUS.

Old words in Natural History seldom become obsolete, but they change their meanings strangely. Were Dioscorides and Pliny *redivivi*, they would find nothing but misnomers! The term *Agaricus*, which anciently applied indiscriminately to all hard coriaceous funguses growing on trees (while the word *Fungus* did imperfect duty for this genus), was next arbitrarily made by Linnæus to stand representative for such only as had gills, " fungi lamellati terrestres et *arborei.*"* Persoon, again, under the name *Amanita* (a Galenic word, but hitherto unappropriated), made a new genus of such Agarics as were invaginated, *i.e.* shut up during the earlier period of their development in a volva; of such as had veins in place of gills, *Merulius;* and of such as had anastomosing gills formed another, *Dædalea,* a third division. More recently, Fries has greatly simplified the study of this very large and difficult genus by eliminating all of a coriaceous texture, and (having restored to it the genus *Amanita*) by then dividing the whole into sections; enabling us to arrive at an accuracy in the discrimination of species which was wholly unattainable before his time. His first grand series of Agarics comprehends those of white spores (Leucospori†), and of this his first section is—

Subgenus 1. Amanita.‡

All the Agarics belonging to this subgenus are, during the immaturity of the fungus, furnished with a volva and a ring; some have a velum in addition, and in this case, the surface of the pileus is covered with warts, or verrucæ. This natural division was adopted long ago by Micheli, who gave the name *Uovoli* to those which had only the first two, and that of *Tignosi* to those that had all three. Altogether they form but a very small group, but one very important to distinguish accurately, as it includes, besides one or two very delicate species, some which are highly poisonous.

* Raii Syn. 2. † λευκὸς, *white,* and σπόρος, a *seed.*
‡ *Ag. ovoides* (Bull.), which is white, and *Ag. Cæsareus* (Scop.), which is red, with yellow gills, belong to this division.

Bot. Char. Pileus at first campanulate, then plane; fleshy towards the centre, attenuated at the margin; *gills* ventricose, narrow behind, free, numerous, at length denticulate, the imperfect ones few, of a determinate form according to the kind, and, with one exception (that of *Ag. Cæsareus*), white. *Stalk* generally enlarged at the base, frequently bulbous, solid, or stuffed with a cotton-like substance, which is at length absorbed; *ring* descending, imperfect, fugacious; *flesh* white, unchanging.

Esculent species: *Ag. vaginatus.*

Of the *Tignosi*, that is, those with warts on their surface, some have striated margins, others are without striæ.

Esculent species: *Ag. rubescens.*

Subgenus 2. Lepiota.*

Bot. Char. Volva fugacious, *veil* single, universal, closely adhering to and confluent with the epidermis, when burst forming a more or less persistent ring towards the middle of the stem; *stem* hollow, stuffed more or less densely with fine arachnoid threads, thickened at the base, fibrillose; *pileus* fleshy, not compact, ovate when young, soon campanulate, then expanded and umbonate, more or less shagged with scales; *flesh* white, soft, sometimes changing colour; *gills* free, unequal, white, never decurrent.

Solitary, persistent, autumnal funguses, growing on the ground. Not dangerous.

Esculent species: *Ag. procerus, Ag. excoriatus.*

Subgenus 3. Armillaria.†

Bot. Char. Veil single, partial, forming a persistent ring, which in the unexpanded plant is joined to the margin of the

---

* λεπìs, a *scale.* † *Armilla*, a *ring.*

pileus;* *stem* solid, firm, subfibrillose, unequal; *pileus* fleshy, convex, expanded, obtuse; *epidermis* entire, even in the scaly species, and not continuous with the fibres of the ring; *flesh* white and firm; *gills* broad, unequal, somewhat acute behind.

Esculent species: *Ag. melleus* (?).

Subgenus 4. LIMACIUM.†

Esculent species: *none*.

Subgenus 5. TRICHOLOMA.‡

Bot. Char. *Veil* fibrous or floccose, fugacious; *stalk* generally solid, firm, fleshy, attenuated upwards, scaly, fibrillose or striate; *pileus* fleshy, compact, campanulate or depressed, convex; margin attenuated, at first involute, shagged with woolly fibres or lanugo; *gills* unequal, obtuse behind, emarginate; *flesh* white and unchangeable.

Esculent species: *Ag. prunulus* and *Ag. personatus*.§

Subgenus 6. RUSSULA‖ (*Scop.*).

Bot. Char. No *veil*; *stem* smooth, equal, glabrous, strong, white, spongy within; *pileus* at first campanulate, then hemispherical, in age depressed, fleshy in the centre, thin at the margin, which is never reflexed at any period of growth, the epidermis bare, smooth, occasionally sticky in wet weather; *gills* juiceless, mostly equal, occasionally forked, the short ones few, rigid, brittle, broad in front, behind narrow, acute,

---

* This ring seems formed by the external fibres of the stalk, which, having reached the posterior extremity of the gills, are reflected backwards to the margin of the pileus when they become attached.

† *Limax*, a *slug*.   ‡ θρίξ, a *hair*, and λῶμα, a *fringe*.

§ Not described by Vittadini among the esculent funguses of Italy, and so probably unknown there.

‖ *Russulus*, red.

properly free but apparently adnato-decurrent, from the effusion of the stem into the pileus; *flesh* firm, dry, white, moderately compact, brittle; *sporules* white or ochraceous; *gills* white or yellow.

Large or middle size, persistent, solitary funguses, growing on the ground.

Esculent species: *Ag. heterophyllus, virescens*, and *ruber*.
Acrid species: *Ag. emeticus, sanguineus*, and *alutaceus*.

Subgenus 7.   GALORRHEUS.*

Bot. Char. No *veil*; *stalk* equal, round, solid, effused into the pileus; *pileus* fleshy, compact, generally umbilicate, margin even, when young involute; *gills* unequal, sometimes very thick, often forked, narrow, attenuated behind, brittle, connected by a prolonged tooth to the stalk, down which they are slightly decurrent; *flesh* firm and juicy, distilling milk.

Esculent species: *Ag. deliciosus* and *piperatus*.

Subgenus 8.   CLYTOCYBE.†

Bot. Char. Veil none; *pileus* at first convex, at length infundibuliform; *gills* unequal. The characteristics of this subgenus are rather negative than positive; many of the contained species vary considerably amongst themselves, but the subdivisions founded on such variations are all well marked.

Subdivision *Dasyphylli*.‡   *Gills* in close juxtaposition, decurrent or acutely adnate.

Esculent species: *Ag. nebularis*.

Subdivision *Camarophylli*.§   *Pileus* subcompact, dry; *gills* very distant, vaulted, decurrent.

Esculent species: *Ag. virgineus*.

---

* γάλα, *milk*, and ῥέω, *to flow*.   † κλίτος, a *declivity*, and κυβή, a *head*.
‡ δασὺς, *thick*, and φύλλον, a *leaf*.   § καμάρα, a *vault*, and φύλλον, a *leaf*.

Subdivision *Chondropodes.** *Pileus* tough, dry, *gills* nearly free, close, white, external coat of stem subcartilaginous.

Esculent species: *Ag. fusipes.*

Subdivision *Scortei.* *Pileus* subcoriaceous; *gills* free, subdistant.

Esculent species: *Ag. oreades.*

Subgenus 9. Collybia.†

Esculent species: *none.*

Subgenus 10. Mycena.‡

Esculent species: *none.*

Subgenus 11. Omphalia.§

Esculent species: *none.*

Subgenus 12. Pleuropus.||

Bot. Char. *Pileus* unequal, eccentric or lateral; *stem*, when present, solid and firm; *gills* unequal, juiceless, unchangeable, acute behind, growing on trees or wood; for the most part innocuous, but two only generally eaten.

Esculent species: *Ag. ostreatus,* in the subdivision *Concharia;* and *Ag. ulmarius,* in the subdivision *Ægeritaria.*

Series 2. HYPORHODEUS.¶

Sporules pale rose-colour.

Subgenus 13. Clitopilus.**

Bot. Char. *Veil* none; *stem* tolerably firm, subequal, dis-

---

* χόνδρος, a *ligament,* and πούς, a *foot.*   † κόλλυβος, a *copper coin.*
‡ μύκης, a *fungus.*   § ὀμφαλὸς, *umbilicus.*
|| πλευρὸν, a *side,* and πούς, a *foot.*   ¶ ὑπὸ, *under,* and ῥόδεος, *rose-coloured.*
** κλίτος, a *declivity,* and πίλος, a *cap.*

tinct from the pileus; *pileus* fleshy, campanulate or convex, at length somewhat plane, dry, regular; *gills* unequal, changing colour as the fungus matures its seed, fixed, or free.

Esculent species: *Ag. orcella.*

Subgenus 14. LEPTONIA.*

Esculent species: *none.*

Subgenus 15. NOLANEA.†

Esculent species: *none.*

Subgenus 16. ECCILIA.‡

Esculent species: *none.*

Series 3. CORTINARIA.§

Sporules reddish-ochre; *veil* arachnoid.

Subgenus 17. TELAMONIA.‖

Esculent species: *none.*

Subgenus 18. INOLOMA.¶

Bot. Char. Veil fugacious, marginal, consisting of free arachnoid threads; *stem* solid, bulbous, fibrillose, more or less diffused into the pileus, fleshy; *pileus* fleshy, convex when young, then expanded, fibrillose, or viscid, regular, juicy; *gills* emarginato-adnexed, broad, changing colour; colour of the gills or pileus violet.

Large autumnal funguses growing on the ground.

Esculent species: *Ag. violaceus.*

---

* λεπτὸς, *slender.* † *Nola,* a *little bell.*
‡ ἐκκοιλόω, *to hollow out.* § *Cortina,* a *veil.*
‖ τελαμών, *lint.* ¶ ἴνὸς, *of a fibre,* λῶμα, a *fringe.*

Subgenus 19. DERMOCYBE.*

Bot. Char. Veil dry, arachnoid, very fugacious; *stem* not truly bulbous, fibrillose, stuffed when young; *pileus* clothed with fibrillæ, rarely with gluten; *gills* rather unequal, broad, close.

Esculent species: *Ag. castaneus.*

Series 4. DERMINUS.

[In the nine subgenera following, from 20 to 28, viz. *Pholiota, Myxacium, Hebeloma, Flammula, Inocybe, Naucoria, Galera, Tapinia,* and *Crepidotus,* there are no esculent species.]

Series 5. PRATELLA.†

Bot. Char. Veil not arachnoid; *gills* changing colour, clouded, at length dissolving; *sporidia* brown-purple.

Subgenus 29. VOLVARIA.

Esculent species: *none.*

Subgenus 30. PSALIOTA.‡

Bot. Char. Veil forming a partial ring-like investment, more or less persistent; *stalk* robust, subequal, distinct from the pileus; *pileus* fleshy, more or less campanulate when young, almost flat when fully expanded; sometimes sticky, sometimes scaly or else fibrillose, sometimes naked; *gills* unequal, free, or connected with the stalk, broad and deepening in colour.

In addition to the ring, some have a very fugacious *volva* or *velum,* some both one and the other.

Esculent species: *Ag. campestris* and *Georgii.*

---

* δέρμα, a *skin*, and κυβη, a *head.*
† *Pratum,* a *pasture.* ‡ ψάλιον, a *ring.*

[In the four next subgenera, from 31 to 34, *Hypholoma, Psilocybe, Psathyra,* and *Coprinarius,* there are no esculent species.]

Subgenus 35. Coprinus.*

Bot. Char. Gills free, unequal, thin, simple, changing colour, at length deliquescent. *Veil* universal, floccose, fugacious; *stem* fistulose, straight, elongated, brittle, subsquamulose, whitish; *pileus* membranaceous, rarely subcarnose, when young ovato-conic, then campanulate, at length torn and revolute, deliquescent, distinct from the stem, clothed with the flocculose fragments of the veil.

Fugacious funguses, growing in rich dungy places or on rotten wood.

Esculent species: *Ag. comatus* and *atramentarius.*

Subgenus 36. Gomphus.

No esculent species.

Genus 2. CANTHARELLUS.†

Bot. Char. These are distinguished from Agarics, which at first sight they resemble, by having veins in place of gills; that is, by having the prolongations of the fibres of the pileus invested in an *undivided,* in place of a divided hymenium, as occurs in Agarics and in the genus *Boletus.* These veins are prominent, ramifying, seldom anastomosing; central, eccentric, or wanting; no investments; dust white.

Esculent species: *C. cibarius.*

[In the next three genera, *Merulius, Schizophyllum,* and *Dædalea,* there are no esculent species.]

* κόπρος, *dung.*   † κάνθαρος, *a cup.*

Genus 6. POLYPORUS.*

Bot. Char. Hymenium concrete with the substance of the pileus, consisting of subrotund pores with thin simple dissepiments.

Esculent species: *P. frondosus.*

Genus 7. BOLETUS.†

Bot. Char. The word *Boletus*, which has at different times, and under different mycologists, been made to represent in turn many very different funguses, is now restricted to such as have a soft flesh, vertical tubes underneath, round or angular, slightly connected together and with the substance of the pileus, open below, and lined by the sporiferous membrane; the cap horizontal, very fleshy, the stalk generally reticulated, some have an investment; the flesh of many changes colour.

They are all innocuous, according to Vittadini, which is not strictly the case, though many species hitherto reputed unwholesome, or worse, appear to lose their bad properties by drying. The kinds generally eaten are *B. edulis* and *scaber*.

Genus 8. FISTULINA.‡

Bot. Char. Hymenium formed of a distinct substance, but concrete with the fibres of the pileus; *tubes* at first wart-like, somewhat remote, radiato-fimbriate, closed; at length approximated, elongated, open.

Esculent species: *F. hepatica.*

---

* πολὺς, *many*, and πόρος, *a pore.*   † βῶλος, *a ball.*
‡ Named from the *fistulous* nature of the hymenium.

Genus 9. HYDNUM.*

Bot. Char. In this genus the under surface presents a series of conical teeth or bristles of unequal length, solid, continuous with the flesh of the pileus and covered entirely by the sporiferous membrane. The species composing it have no investments; the *flesh* is dry, frequently corky or coriaceous; the *pileus* irregular in shape, and its margin arched and undulated. There are no dangerous species, but which to eat must depend upon the united consent of the stomach and of the teeth.

Esculent species: *H. repandum.*

[In the last five genera of this tribe, namely, *Sistotrema, Irpex, Radulum, Phlebia,* and *Thelephora,* there are no esculent species.]

Tribe 2. *CLAVATI.*†

Hymenium above, smooth; *receptacle* club-shaped or cylindrical, with no distinct margin; *substance* fleshy.

Genus 15. CLAVARIA.

Bot. Char. Receptacle erect, homogeneous, smooth, not distinguishable from the stalk, simple or entirely covered by the hymenium.

All the species in this genus are good to eat.

[In the remaining six genera of this tribe there are no esculent species.]

---

* ὕδνον, a *truffle,* etc.   † *Clava,* a *club.*

Tribe 3. *MITRATI.*

Receptacle **bullate, pileiform,** margined; *hymenium* **superior, never closed.**

Genus 22. MORCHELLA.

Bot. Char. Receptacle **hollow and confluent with stalk, club-shaped,** or, like the pileus, fissured **above with** lacunæ more or less deep, limited by thick folds, anastomosed with reticulations, entirely covered with sporiferous membrane; *flesh* waxy in **texture**; *stalk* constant.

There are two esculent kinds, *M. esculenta* and *semilibera*; the *esculenta* and *hybrida* of Sowerby.

Genus 23. HELVELLA.

Bot. Char. Substance fleshy; *margins* **sinuous;** only the upper **portion of the pileus** sporiferous.

Esculent species: *H. crispa, lacunosa,* and *esculenta.*

[In Genera 24 to 26 there are no esculent species.]

Tribe 4. *CUPULATI.*

Hymenium concrete, **superior, smooth, shut in** while young by the margins of the receptacle; *sporules* disseminated with elasticity **or otherwise**; *receptacle* bowl-shaped, flat or concave; some of this tribe when young have an involucrum.

Genus 27. PEZIZA.

Series ALEURIA. Subgenus MEGALOPYXIS.

Esculent species: *P. acetabulum.*

[In Genera 28 to 45, which conclude the first great division, *Hymenomycetes*, there are no esculent species.]

Division II. GASTEROMYCETES.

Bot. Char. The *receptacle* a close cavity with or without a hymenium; *spores* at last free and variously disseminated.

[In Genera 46 to 73 there are no esculent species.]

Genus 74. BOVISTA.*

Bot. Char. Peridium papyraceous, furnished with a distinct back, which at length peels off altogether, fertile within; *capillitium* equal.

Esculent species: *B. plumbea.*

Genus 75. LYCOPERDON.

Bot. Char. A sessile *peridium*, membranaceous; at first filled with a white, consistent, homogeneous substance, which after a time is converted into a dust of various hues, and is interspersed with copious filaments. The funguses of this genus are invested in two membranes; the innermost of which, or *peridium*, is tough and smooth on the outside, shaggy with floccose threads within. The external membrane, which is very fragile and tender, frequently falls off during the maturation of the seed, which then escapes through the peridium by an irregular orifice at the apex.

Esculent species: *L. plumbeum* and *Bovista.*

---

* Name Latinized from the German *Bofist.*

AGARICUS PRUNULUS, *Vitt.*

PLATE I. FIG. 1.

Subgenus TRICHOLOMA, *Fries.* Subdivision PERSONATA, *ibid.*

AGARICUS MOUCERON, *Bulliard. Casalpinus*, p. 617.
MOUCERON GRIS, *Paulet, Persoon.*

"Cogitatione ante pascuntur succincis novaculis aut argenteo apparatu comitante."—*Pliny.*

"Tout ce qui fait l'ornement des festins s'embaume du parfum de ces cryptogames."—*Persoon.*

Bot. Char. Gregarious, or growing in rings* on the ground; *pileus* thick, convex, irregular in shape, more or less tuberculated, sometimes lobed;† margin not striate, wavy, expanding unequally; *epidermis* cream-coloured, grey, reddish, or of a dirty nankeen hue, paler towards the circumference, soft to the touch like kid, minutely tomentose, fragile, dry, firmly attached to the flesh; flesh firm, compact; *gills* watery, white, very numerous, irregular, with many smaller ones (from 5–11, *Vitt.*) interposed, lying over each other like the plaits of a frill, adnato-emarginate,‡ the imperfect gills rounded off at their posterior end. *Stem* white, robust, firm, solid, somewhat irregular in form, generally thickened at the base, constantly so in young specimens, but in older ones,

---

* They are reproduced in these rings about the same time every year, the circle continuing to enlarge till it breaks up at last into irregular lines, which is a sure sign to the collector that the *Prunulus* is about to disappear from that place, just as the presence of an unbroken ring is conclusive of a plentiful harvest the next spring.

† These lobes, formed by the constriction of the pileus, whilst emerging from the roots of the grass, are sometimes so much strangulated as to present the appearance of small stalkless Agarics growing from the large, and projecting from their sides like ears.

‡ That is, connected by a tooth to the end of the stalk, and not running down it.

though occasionally bulging, it presents not unfrequently an equal cylinder throughout, and sometimes tapers slightly downwards. The fibres are effused into the pileus, spreading out like a fan through its substance; *smell* strong, *taste* agreeable; *spores* white, elliptical, adhering firmly to the body on which they fall. The dried plant retains much the same form it had when fresh.

On tracing this fungus to its origin, (spring is the only time, and the borders of the woodlands the proper place, to look for it,) if we dig up the earth where it grows, this will be found mouldy to a considerable depth beneath the surface, and strongly impregnated with the peculiar odour which the *Prunulus* exhales; this apparent mouldiness being, in fact, the spawn, amidst the white filaments of which many minute Agarics, in various stages of their development, may be found; some, in the earliest, presenting merely white cones destitute of heads, whilst in others a slight protuberance indicates the future pileus forming or already formed. The pileus is at first almost spherical, and involute in its borders, the gills whitish, very minute, and so thickly set as to press one against the other, each communicating to the membrane that lines the next the impressions of its own fibres, which remain in the form of transverse striæ, and furnish a characteristic to this fungus retained during all its subsequent growth (*Vitt.*). The greatest size which I have known the *Prunulus* attain has been in England, where I have picked specimens measuring six inches across, and weighing between four and five ounces; as to the fecundity of this fungus, I collected this spring, from a single ring on the War-Mount at Keston (Kent), from ten to twelve pounds, and in the one field from twenty to twenty-five pounds. In this neighbourhood they are generally destroyed, as injurious to his grass-crops, by the over-careful farmer, quite ignorant, of course, of their value; to which the following extract from a letter of Professor Balbi to Persoon bears testimony:—" This rare and most delicious Agaric, the *Mouceron* of Bulliard, and the *Ag. prunulus* of other authors, abounds on the hills above the valley of **Stafora**, near **Bobbio**, where it is called Spinaroli, and is in great request; the country people eat it fresh in a variety of ways, or they dry and sell it for from twelve to sixteen francs a pound." Vittadini says, truly enough, that the fresh is better than the dried *Prunulus*, the substance of the latter being rather coriaceous, but the gravy prepared from it in this state, being very rich and well-flavoured, is largely used by those who reject the body of the mushroom; three or four thrown into a pot of the lighter broths or of beef-tea render them more savoury. To dry the *Prunulus* it is usual to cut it into four or more pieces, which are exposed for some days to a dry air and then threaded: it acquires an aroma by the process, and communicates this to any dish of which it is afterwards an ingredient.

It would be extremely difficult to confound this Agaric with any other; its mode of growth in circles, the extreme narrowness of its gills, which are moreover striate, the thickness of its pileus, and the bulging character of its stalk, would render a mistake almost impossible, even did it grow in autumn when other funguses abound, in place of appearing only in spring when few species comparatively abound.

The best mode of cooking the *Ag. prunulus* is either in a mince or fricassee it with any sort of meat, or in a *vol-au-vent*, the flavour of which it greatly improves; or simply prepared with salt, pepper, and a small piece of bacon, lard, or butter, to prevent burning, it constitutes of itself a most excellent dish. It has the great advantage of appearing in spring, at a season the common mushroom never occurs. I have placed it first in the series of Plates, as being the most savoury fungus with which I am acquainted.*

When eaten alone, Sterbeck's white mustard will be found an excellent condiment for it; this is prepared as follows:— Bruise in a mortar some sweet almonds with a little water, then add salt, pepper, and some lemon-juice, rub together till the whole is of the consistence of common mustard.

AGARICUS PROCERUS, *Scop.*
Plate II.
Subgenus Lepiota, *Fries.*

"Elle est d'une saveur très-agréable et d'une chair tendre, très-délicate et très-bonne à manger. Les amateurs la préfèrent même au champignon de couche, comme ayant une chair plus fine et étant beaucoup plus légère sur l'estomac."—*Paulet.*

This, which is one of the most delicate funguses, fortunately is not rare in England. In Italy it is in equal request with the *Amanita Cæsarea*; in France it is also in high esteem,—" servie sur toutes les tables, elle est bonne à toute sauce" (*Thore*); and were its excellent qualities better known here, they could not fail to secure it a general reception into our best kitchens, and a frequent place among our side-dishes at table. The beauty and remarkable appearance of this Agaric have procured for it a variety of names: *colubrinus*, from the snake-like markings on the stem; *clypeatus*, from

---

* The *Prunulus* is much prized in the Roman market, where it easily fetches 30 baiocchi, *i.e.* 15*d.* per lb.; a large sum for any luxury at Rome. It is sent in little baskets as presents to patrons, fees to medical men, and bribes to Roman lawyers. When dried, it constitutes the so-called " Funghi di Genoa," which are sold on strings throughout Italy.

its umbonated top; '*fungo parasole*,' from the orbicular form of the wide-spread pileus; and *Gambaltiem* or *Fonz de la gamba lunga*, from the extraordinary height of the stalk. Autumn is the time of its greatest abundance, but individual specimens occur occasionally throughout the summer.

It grows solitary or few together in hedgebanks and pasture-grounds.

The pileus, which is commonly from four to four and a half inches across, sometimes attains a width of six or seven. At first it is concealed in a volva, but breaking from this it goes through a variety of forms, from that of an ovoid cone to that of a flattened disk. It is umbonated at the centre, and covered with scales, which are formed by the breaking up of the mud-coloured epidermis, and are large, raised, and persistent at the centre; thin, regular, and lighter in hue at the circumference, "the whole surface resembling a delightfully soft, shaggy-brown leather" (*Purton*). The flesh of the pileus is white and cottony, that of the stalk fibrous and somewhat brittle, with a subrubescent tinge, the whole plant turning to a rufous-orange when bruised; the gills are of a pale flesh-colour, occasionally forked, ventricose, denticulate, remote from the stalk, and having a circular pit between it and their central extremities, which are fixed into a kind of collar. The stalk tawny, striped circularly with bands of white, formed by the breaking up of the epidermis; is bulbous at the base and attenuated upwards; its apex rounded, and penetrating deeply through the flesh of the pileus (which receives it as in a socket), gives rise to the central umbo on the upper surface of the cap. The ring moveable, like that of an umbrella-stick, broad, compact, membranaceous immediately round the stalk, and fibrous towards its free margin, is white above and tawny or of the same colour as the stalk on its under surface. The smell is like that of newly-ground meal; the taste is pleasant; the spores are white and elliptic.

The *Ag. excoriatus* resembles the *Ag. procerus* very closely, but is easily distinguished from it by its smaller size, the absence of the bulb at the base of the stalk, and the ring being often attached instead of free.

Being equally esculent, the following receipts will serve for both :—

"Comme il est très-léger et très-délicat, il faut le faire sauter dans l'huile fine après l'avoir assaisonné d'un point d'ail, de poivre et de sel ; en quelques instants il est cuit. On le mange aussi en fricassée de poulet, cuit sur le gril ou dans la tourtière avec de beurre, de fines herbes, du poivre, du sel, et de la chapelure de pain ; on ne mange point la tige, elle est d'une texture coriace" (*Roques*).

The ketchup from both kinds is better than that procured from the *Agaricus campestris*, or common mushroom.

N.B.—I have in the above notice described one variety of *Agaricus procerus*; there is, however, if not another, at least a remarkable modification of this, in which the pileus is thinner and much less shaggy, the gills less broad but similar in shape, the stalk more slender and elongate. This variety is also nearly void of odour, *and its flesh does not change colour on being bruised:* for culinary purposes this distinction is without importance, as both are equally good.

BOLETUS EDULIS, *Bulliard*.

Plate III. Figs. 1 and 2.

Section Cortinaria, *Fries*.

"Atto sovra ognun altro fungo al commercio, forma da questo lato, per non pochi paesi della Lombardia, una delle principali risorsi della povera gente."—*Vitt*.

The ancient Romans were well acquainted with this truly

delicious fungus, and in general appear to have done it justice; the strings of dried Suillus, which his countrymen, on the testimony of Pliny, were in the habit of fetching from Bithynia, were in all likelihood the same as those similarly-prepared strings of the modern Porcino which are sold during the winter in every market-place throughout Italy.* Vittadini mentions a curious fact respecting them, viz. that though they are composed of many different Boletuses, no mischief was ever known to originate from their indiscriminate and very extensive consumption; whence he concludes that *all* the species of this genus are innocuous, or, at least, that drying and cooking will extract any deleterious principles which they may have originally contained;—an inference, he thinks, supported by the daily use among the peasantry of certain districts of the *B. luridus*, which of all bad Boletuses commonly passes for the worst, and by his having experimented with it in large doses upon animals, who did not suffer in consequence. I have eaten in England a small quantity both of *B. Grevillei* and of *B. granulatus*, which have much of the flavour of the *B. edulis*; of the *B. subtomentosus* (though, on the authority of Trattinick, it is eaten in Germany) I have no personal experience, nor do I recommend to the amateur any species beyond the two universally eaten and approved of on the Continent, viz.:—*B. edulis* and *B. scaber*.

B. edulis.—Bot. Char. *Pileus* from six to seven inches across, pulvinate, smooth, with a thick margin, varying in colour from light brown or bronze, to bay, dark brown, or

* If the Suillus be indeed the same as the modern Porcino, as its name would imply, few who know how good it is will be disposed to pity Martial, who laments his hard case, in having had to eat this fungus at his patron's table, while he feasted on the Boletus, *i.e.* the *Ag. Cæsareus*. It would seem however from this epigram, that the Suillus was not in Martial's time, what it now unquestionably is, a favourite with the rich.

black, or a mixture of all these colours. The epidermis firmly adherent to the flesh, that firm, and except the part in immediate contact with the skin, which has a slight brown tint, white; the under surface of the cap nearly flat, often presenting a circular pit or depression round the stalk; *tubes* at first white, then yellow, lastly of an olive or yellow-green tint, in the earlier stage of development (their free extremities then lie against the side of the stalk) closed; afterwards, as the cap expands, stopped up with a waxy-looking material of a dirty pearl colour. *Stem* varying much in shape at different periods of the growth of the *Boletus*, always thick and solid; at first white, but soon changing to fawn colour, beautifully meshed or mapped (especially on its upper portion) with reticulations characteristic of this species. As the period for casting its seed advances, the inferior surface of the cap swells out, the waxy matter is absorbed, the tubes present deep and rounded orifices to the eye, and presently emit an abundant seminal dust, of an ochraceous green hue (sometimes difficult to collect, from the quantity of moisture exhaled with it), after which both cap and stalk become flaccid, the tubes turn to a dirty green, and the whole fungus falls rapidly into a state of decomposition. The favourite sites for this *Boletus* are woods, especially those of pines, oaks, and chestnuts; it abounds in autumn, but occurs in spring and occasionally in summer. There is one variety, the *pinicola*, whose name gives its whereabouts, which differs from the foregoing, in having a moist, somewhat sticky cap, a watery flesh changing near the tubes to a light yellow-green when bruised; the reticulations are ill-marked in this species.

The *Boletus edulis* cannot be mistaken for any other *Boletus* because it alone presents all the following characters united, viz. a cap of which the surface is smooth; tubes the colour of which varies with each period of its growth, beautiful and singular reticulations of the stalk, especially towards the upper portion, and a flesh which is white and unchanging.

The *Boletus castaneus*, which bears some little general resemblance to it, is at once distinguished by having a cottony fibrillose stem without reticulations, a downy cap and dirty yellow dust: neither can it be confounded with the *B. subtomentosus* nor *B. luridus*, because in addition to many other points of difference, both these change colour on being cut or bruised.

As to the best manner of cooking *B. edulis*, this must be left to the taste of the gourmet; in every way it is good. Its tender and juicy flesh, its delicate and sapid flavour, render it equally acceptable to the plain and to the accomplished cook. It imparts a relish alike to the homely hash and the dainty ragoût, and may be truly said to improve every dish of which it is a constituent. "Nihil tetigit quod non ornavit." "Though much neglected in this country, it appears to be a most valuable article of food. It resembles much in taste the common mushroom, and is quite as delicate; it abounds in seasons when these are not to be found." (*Berkeley*.)

Modes of Cooking Boletus edulis. (PERSOON.)

It may be cooked in white sauce, with or without chicken, in fricassee broiled or baked with butter, salad oil, pepper, salt, chopped herbs, and bread-crumbs; to which some add ham or a mince of anchovy. It makes excellent fritters: some roast it with onions (basting with butter), but as these take longer to cook than the *Boletus*, this must not be put down till the onions have begun to soften.

Boletus edulis Soup, made in Hungary. (PAULET.)

Having dried some *Boletuses* in an oven, soak them in

tepid water, thickening with toasted bread, till the whole be of the consistence of a *purée*, then rub through a sieve, throw in some stewed *Boletuses*, boil together, and serve with the usual condiments.

AGARICUS CAMPESTRIS.

Section PRATELLA.   Subdivision PSALIOTA, *Fries*.

AGARICUS CAMPESTRIS, *Linn.*

> "Où croit ce champignon, délice des festins,
> Que l'art fait chaque jour naître dans nos jardins."—*Castel.*

There is scarcely any one in England who does not feel himself competent to decide on the genuineness of a mushroom : its pink gills are carefully separated from those of a kindred fungus *Ag. Georgii*, which are of a flesh-coloured grey, and out of the pickings of ten thousand hands, a mistake is of rare occurrence ; and yet no fungus presents itself under such a variety of forms, of such singular diversities of aspect ! the inference is plain ; less discrimination than that employed to distinguish this, would enable any who should take the trouble, to recognize at a glance many of those esculent species, which every spring and autumn fill our plantations and pastures with plenteousness. Neither is this left to be a mere matter of inference ; it is corroborated in a singular manner by what takes place at Rome ; here, whilst many hundred baskets of what we call toadstools are carried home for the table, almost the only one condemned to be thrown into the Tiber, by the inspector of the fungus market is our own mushroom :* indeed, in such dread is this held in the Papal

---

* " Il Sorvegliatore fa gettare ai venditori tutti i funghi fracidi e quelli che crede nocivi, ed è assolutamente proibita la vendita dei così detti prateroli buoni o cattivi che sieno."—*Sanguinetti* (extract from an unpublished letter).

States, that no one knowingly would touch it. " It is reckoned one of their fiercest imprecations," writes Professor Sanguinetti, "amongst our lower orders, infamous for the horrible nature of their oaths, to pray that any one may die of a *Pratiolo*;" and although it has been some years registered among the esculent funguses of Milan and Pavia (on the authority of Vittadini), it has not yet found its way into those markets. Besides the general botanical characters which apply to all varieties of *Ag. campestris*, almost every writer has felt the necessity of pointing out several peculiarities, belonging to each. Common to all are a fleshy pileus, which is sometimes smooth, sometimes scaly, in colour white, or of different shades of tawny, fuliginous, or brown; gills free, at first pallid, then flesh-coloured, then pink, next purple, at length tawny-black; the stem white, full, firm, varying in shape, furnished with a white persistent ring; the spores brown-black, and a volva which is very fugacious.

Var. A. *edulis.*

This, which is our button mushroom, lies at first concealed in the earth, at which period it presents the appearance of a puff-ball; at a second stage of its growth, it exhibits a white, smooth, and continuous epidermis; gills rounded off at their posterior end; a large, somewhat funnel-shaped, *double* ring, free, and somewhat moveable on the stem, which is short and thick. This, according to Vittadini, is the most sapid variety of any.

Var. B. *pratensis.*

This differs from the last in the duskier hue of its pileus, which is moreover scaly, and has ragged margins; the gills are ventricose; and the ring, which is subfugacious, is cortinarious, *i. e.* of a cobweb texture, and reflexed; the stalk is longer than in the last species, and tapers towards the base; the colour of the flesh in this variety is vinous or even sanguine.

Var. c. silvicola.

This differs from the two former in the following particulars; the gills are *pallid*, taper *equally* at both ends, and come off at a considerable distance from the stalk, which is surrounded above by a very delicate ring, and is *bulbous* at the base, the bulb showing traces of the volva.*

Var. D. anceps.

Such *uncultivated* mushrooms as when eaten even in small quantity, produce violent derangement of the stomach and intestinal canal, belong to a variety which, since it grows under hedges, is sometimes called "the hedge mushroom;" this, to which, for distinction's sake, I have given the name of *anceps*, is by no means of rare occurrence. In order to discriminate it properly from the wholesome varieties, the first point to notice is its extreme lightness as compared with its bulk, that the gills are of a deeper and of a more lurid red than those of *var. edulis*, and in age less purple; they are also less deliquescent. The flesh is more tough and not so juicy. The stem, as in the *var. silvicola*, is curved and bulbous, but also fistulose throughout. The ring complete, firm, broad, reflexed, and *persistent*; the odour disagreeable, and the taste insipid. The form of the pileus that of an obtuse cone in young specimens; extremely flat in the middle state; and more or less concave in age. It seldom grows solitary. The mushroom

---

* "This is that variety of *Ag. campestris* which has been so often confounded with the *Amanita verna*, and with these the *Ag. albus virosus*; all these funguses, besides presenting a strong similarity in appearance, are found in the same locality, and at about the same time of year."—*Vitt.*

proper, like other funguses, should be eaten fresh; a few hours making all the difference between its wholesomeness or unwholesomeness: nor need this surprise us when we consider how many principles enter into its composition, how short is the period of its existence, and how liable it must be to enter into new combinations in consequence. Vauquelin found in its flesh fat, adipocere, osmazome, an animal matter insoluble in alcohol, sugar, fungine, and acetate of potash. What a medley! and what wonder, if the changes induced during decomposition should cause the indigestions suffered by those who have eaten them in this state! The mushroom, having the same proximate principles as meat, requires, like meat, to be cooked before these become changed. The *Ag. campestris* may be prepared in a great variety of ways: they give a fine flavour to soups, and greatly improve beef-tea;—where arrow-root and weak broths are distasteful to the patient, the simple seasoning of a little ketchup will frequently form an agreeable change. Some roast them, basting with melted butter and white (French) wine sauce.* In patties and *vols-au-vent* they are equally excellent; in fricassees, as everybody knows, they are the important element of the dish. Roques recommends in all cases the removal of the gills before dressing, which though it secures a more elegant-looking *entremet*, is only flattering the eye at the expense of the palate.

Var. E. bovinus.

This variety differs from the *Ag. Georgii* and the type of the species in size and other particulars. There are specimens which measure fifteen inches across the pileus, with a stalk of corresponding dimensions. The pileus is shaggy, like that of

* Ude complains that we have none of the light French wines for sauces except champagne. Cider or perry will, however, be found good substitutes.

the *Ag. procerus,* with epidermic scales, which are at first nearly white, but in fully developed specimens, of a rich tawny colour, like the *Polyporus squamosus;* and sometimes of a red-brown. The scales more depressed than in *Ag. procerus,* the gills not ventricose, equal at both ends, separated from the stalk by a fossa or groove which runs round its apex; the stalk solid, attenuated at the very base, but thickened just above it, a slightly vinous hue when bruised; flesh of ring perfect, persistent, and hanging round the stalk like a sheet of thin white kid; into which a number of delicate silver threads may be traced proceeding from the apex of stem. The smell is powerful but agreeable, as also is the flavour; no part of the surface ever turns yellow. This variety is both wholesome and well-flavoured; as it is commonly known by the peasants under the name of the "Ox-Mushroom," I have called it *bovinus.*

Receipt I.—"*A la Provençale.*"

Steep for two hours in oil, with some salt, pepper, and a little garlic: then toss up in a small stewpan over a brisk fire, with parsley chopped and a little lemon-juice.

Receipt II.—*To stuff Mushrooms.*

Take large mushrooms, full-grown, but not black; remove the gills, and place in lieu of them the following stuffing:—bacon shredded, crumbs of bread, chopped herbs, and a little garlic or eschalots (as for omelettes), salt, pepper, and a taste of spice. Broil in paper as a Maintenon cutlet, moistening with butter when necessary.

Receipt III.—*Mushrooms "à la Marquis Cussi."*

Take button mushrooms; put to them a very small quantity of garlic, finely chopped; toss up over a brisk fire with a little butter; add some lemon-juice; give them a few turns; then add salt, pepper, nutmeg, and a wine-glassful of the richest brown gravy (Grande Espagnole); when the mushrooms are warmed through in this, add a couple of glasses of Sauterne, simmer for ten minutes, and serve.

A homely mode of cooking *Ag. campestris* in Bucks. is to cut up the buttons with pieces of bacon the size of dice, and then to boil them in a dumpling.

Method of Cultivating.

The following method of cultivating mushrooms is given in Paxton's 'Botanical Dictionary:'—

"Collect a sufficient quantity of fresh horse-droppings, as free from straw as possible; lay it in an open shed in a heap or ridge; here it will heat violently, and in consequence should be now and then turned for sweetening; after this has subsided to moderation, it will be in a fit state for forming into a bed. In the process of making the bed, the dung should be put on in small quantities and beat firmly and equally together, until it is the required size; in this state let it remain until the highest degree of heat to which it is capable of coming is ascertained, which may be readily done by inserting a heat-stick, and pressing it with the hand; if not found violent, the spawn may be broken up into pieces of two or three inches square, and put into holes about three inches in depth by six inches asunder, over its surface; after this, throw a very small quantity of well-broken droppings over the whole. In this state let it remain for two or three weeks, when a loamy soil may be put on about an inch or an inch and a half thick, and gently patted with the spade. If the temperature of the house be kept about sixty or sixty-five degrees, mushrooms may be expected in six weeks. It is not well to water the beds much, particularly when bearing; it is much better to throw a little water over the path and flues, which will both improve the colour and the flavour of the mushrooms, without being attended with those bad effects frequently resulting from watering, viz. that of destroying the young stock, and turning browner those already fit for table."—*Paxton's Bot. Dict.*

With regard to the spawn, it may be collected as recommended in the French work cited by M. Roques, and kept in a dry place till wanted; or by digging about the roots of growing mushrooms, and carrying away the earth which contains it. The *débris* of a former mushroom-bed will always furnish spawn for a new.

AGARICUS EXQUISITUS, *nob.*

Plate IV., Figs. 3, 4, and 5.

Section Psaliota, *Fries.*   Subdivision Pratella, *ibid.*

Agaricus Georgii, *Withering.*

"L'Agarico esquisito è un fungo sano, oltremodo delicato e di facilissima digestione."—*Vitt.*

"Its flavour is far inferior to that of the common mushroom."—*Berkeley.*

This fungus, called also the Horse Mushroom, from the enormous dimensions* to which it sometimes attains, is for the most part shunned by the English epicure; it is also this species from which many persons report themselves to have

---

* "Hopkirk records an instance of one weighing five pounds six ounces, and measuring forty-three inches in circumference. Withering mentions another that weighed fourteen pounds."—*Berkeley.*

suffered indigestion attended with violent colicky pains, when they have eaten it by mistake for the *Ag. campestris*. It is sold, under the name of White Caps, for making ketchup; but, notwithstanding its foreign name and reputation, most persons will agree with Mr. Berkeley, in holding both its flesh and its juices as greatly inferior to those of the *Ag. campestris*. Our other name for it, that of St. George's Agaric, can have no reference to the time of its appearance, as it is seldom met with in England till after that saint's day; it has, moreover, the same name in Hungary, where the inhabitants look upon it as a special gift from Saint George.

Its botanical characters are the following:—

Pileus at first conico-campanulate, covered with floccose shreds, which are very fugacious; when fully expanded, minutely squamulose, of a beautiful white, shining and smooth; turning yellow when bruised, and sometimes exuding a yellow juice (Sibthorpe). *Gills* numerous, broad, attenuated both ways, but most so behind, free, of a pallid hue (grey flesh-colour), during the growth of the fungus; later, clouded brown-black; the imperfect gills obtuse behind. *Stem* long, subcylindrical, slightly thickened at the base, white without, stuffed within. *Ring* tumid and reflected over the stalk. *Flesh* of both pileus and stalk compact, fibrous, and fragile. Flavour and smell strong, and, according to Vittadini, agreeable, but according to English perception generally the reverse. Persoon pronounces this fungus to be *superior* to the common mushroom in smell, taste, and digestibility, on which accounts, he says, it is generally preferred in France. It is to be cooked in the same way as that, and, if eaten in moderation, will seldom be found to incommode the stomach or offend the palate.

Locality.—Pastures, amidst thickets, under trees, generally in large rings, reproducing itself every year in the same situations.

AGARICUS DELICIOSUS.

PLATE V., FIG. 4.

Orange Milk Agaric.

Subgenus GALORRHEUS.

Bot. Char. Gregarious. *Pileus* from three to four inches across; colour dull orange-rufous, frequently zoned with concentric circles of a brighter hue, fleshy, firm, full of red orange milk, which turns green on exposure to the air (as does the whole plant when bruised); the margin at first involute and downy, then expanded, afterwards depressed. *Gills* decurrent, forked at the base, always of the same colour as the pileus, rather distant, substantial. *Stem* from two to three inches high, slightly bent, stuffed in part, scrobiculate (*i. e.* marked with little superficial pits); at the base strigose (*i. e.* covered with short pointed hairs).

This is one of the best Agarics with which I am acquainted, fully deserving both its *name* and the estimation in which it is held abroad. Its flesh is firm, juicy, sapid, and nutritious. It grows under old Scotch firs and pines, and occasionally in considerable abundance, and is well worth the trouble of searching for from September to the beginning of November, when it is in season. There is but one fungus which it in any way resembles, and as that one (*Ag. torminosus*) is acrid and poisonous, the gatherer must pay particular attention to the following characteristic difference between the two, viz. that the milk of the *Ag. deliciosus* is *red and subsequently turus green*, while that of the *Ag. torminosus* is *white* and unchangeable.

Mr. Sowerby thus speaks in praise of this species:—" I had one dressed; it was very luscious eating, full of rich gravy, with a little of the flavour of mussels."

Sir James Smith, in his 'Tour,' says:—" The market of Marseilles exhibited a prodigious quantity of *Ag. deliciosus*, which really deserves its name, being the most delicious mushroom known."

The *Agaricus deliciosus* may be served with a white sauce, or fried; but the best way to cook them, after duly seasoning with pepper and salt, and putting a piece of butter upon each, is to bake (in a closely-covered pie-dish) for about three-quarters of an hour.

BOLETUS SCABER, *Fries*.
Plate VI. Figs. 1, 2.

"Fungo innocente e che non può cagionare alcun danno, non molto ricercato a motivo, senza dubbio, del cambiamento di colore in cui va soggetto la sua carne allorchè viene rotta o compressa."—*Vitt*.

Bot. Char. This fungus presents itself under two distinct forms; in the first, the *B. aurantiacus* of Bull., the *pileus* (generally rather downy, but sometimes rough) is of a beautiful deep orange hue; in the other it is cinereous.

In both cases its shape is that of a hemisphere of from three to seven inches across, the surface of which becomes viscid when moist, and is minutely downy. In the first variety, the *stem* is rough with black, in the second with orange scales.

Half a foot is its average height; it is attenuated upwards. While young, it is very thick in proportion to the pileus, and exhibits frequently the traces of a floccose veil. The flesh is thick and flabby, of a dingy white, not greatly changeable in young specimens, but deepening in colour when old, and acquiring a vinous tint;* the *tubes* are of a dirty white, those that surround the stem being shorter than the rest.

The odour of this fungus is slight; the taste subacid; the seminal dust copious, and tawny-ferruginous. It may be cooked like the *B. edulis*, and has an agreeable flavour; but being more viscid in substance, it requires when stewed to be thinned with water; when dried, it loses all odour, and is then insipid and unfit for food.

BOLETUS LURIDUS.

Plate VI. Figs. 3, 4, and 5.

Nothing can be more accurate than Mr. Berkeley's description of this species, which I therefore subjoin:—" Woods. Summer and autumn. Common. *Pileus* two to six inches broad, convex, expanded, minutely tomentose, olive, brick-red, pinkish, cream-coloured, or ferruginous-brown. *Flesh* more or less yellow, changing to blue.† *Tubes* free, yellow

---

* "It is commonly supposed that such funguses as change colour afford thereby a clear evidence of their noxious properties, and yet daily experience, as far as it went, ought to have led to just the opposite conclusion. Almost all the poisonous Agarics have a flesh that does *not* change colour, and we know as yet of no Boletus, many of which *do* so change, that is really unsafe to eat."—*Vitt.*

† This blue loses much of its intensity by long exposure to the air. It is moreover to be remarked that in specimens, the flesh of which has been eaten into by slugs or insects, no change of colour takes place.

or greenish; their orifices of a beautiful red or bright orange, quite simple, round. *Spores* olivaceous-ochre. *Stem* very variable in length, bulbous, tomentose, sometimes quite smooth, red with ferruginous or the brightest yellow shades, solid, generally more or less marked or reticulated with crimson-red, *very deleterious*" (? *).

AGARICUS PERSONATUS.

Plate I. Fig. 2.

Subgenus Tricholoma, *Fries.*

Blewitts.

I never met with this fungus in Italy; it has not been described by Vittadini, nor, that I am aware of, by any Italian mycologist; neither is it mentioned by Cordier or Roques, in their treatises on the esculent funguses of France. Extremely common in England, this species has already found its way to Covent Garden, where, according to Sowerby, it is sold under the name of "Blewitts."† The favourite haunt of the Blewitt is amidst grass, where it grows in clusters, or in large rings, seldom appearing before October.

The botanical characters, as given by Mr. Berkeley, are as follows :—" *Pileus* from two to six inches broad, fleshy, firm; pale bistre or purple-lilac, occasionally violet; convex, obtuse, very smooth, and shining, as if oiled, but not viscid; margin involute, pulverulento-tomentose. *Gills* rounded; free, narrow in front, paler than the pileus, sometimes violet, turning

---

* This requires further corroboration.

† Sc. "Blue Hats" (?), as *Ag. Georgii* is called "White Caps," and *Ag. Oreades* "Scotch Bonnets."

to a dirty flesh-colour, especially when bruised; *stem* from one to three inches high, three-quarters of an inch thick, firm, bulbous, solid, mottled within towards the apex, with watery spots; clothed more or less with villous fibrillæ, tinged with violet; odour like that of *Oreades*, but rather overpowering; taste pleasant." As the "Blewitt" is apt to imbibe in wet weather a great quantity of moisture, it should not be gathered during rain; when not water-soaked it is a fine firm fungus with a flavour of veal, like which it is to be dressed *en papillottes* with savoury herbs and the usual condiments, and the more highly seasoned the better.

AGARICUS OREADES, *Bolt.*

Plate VII. Fig. 4.

Subgenus CLITOCYBE.   Section SCORTEI, *Fries.*

Scotch Bonnets.

Every one knows the Champignon,—that little buff fungus which during so many months in the year comes up in successive crops, in great profusion after rain, and generally in rings. These Champignons abound everywhere: this summer (1847) Hyde Park was full of them; amid the seared and much-trodden grass they were continually tracing their fairy rings, and in some instances they reached the very border of the gravel walks. Independent of the excellent flavour of this little mushroom, which is as good as that of most funguses, two circumstances give it an additional value in a domestic point of view, viz. the facility with which it is dried, and its very extensive dissemination. When dried (two or three days' exposure to the air is generally sufficient to effect this), the *Ag. oreades* may be kept for years without losing any of its aroma or goodness, which on the contrary become improved by the process, so as, in fact, to impart more flavour to the dish than would have been imparted by the fresh fungus; though it is not to be denied that the flesh then becomes coriaceous and less easy of digestion.* From the sad accidents occasioned by persons mistaking other small and poisonous Agarics growing in the neighbourhood of the Champignon for the Champignon itself, this species is frequently looked upon with suspicion, and not often eaten in England. The Agaric the least unlike and most commonly found growing in company with the *Ag. oreades*, is the *Ag. semilobatus*, which is nearly allied to, if it be not the same as the *Ag. virosus* of Sowerby. But as I have also heard of a gentleman who intending to gather Champignons, and taking home some *Ag. dryophilus* by mistake, was rendered very ill by his repast, to prevent the recurrence of such mistakes for the future, I here add the botanical characters, marking what is peculiar to each in italics. *Ag. dryophilus* is represented in Pl. VII. fig. 5.

AG. DRYOPHILUS.

Solitary or tufted. Pileus from one to two inches broad, whitish, pinkish, yellowish, or yellow-brown, flat, sometimes *depressed*, fleshy, thin, *fragile, when moist easily injured*, of a tougher substance when dry. Gills soft, tender, numerous, white, or pale yellow straw-colour. Stem shining, *hollow*, of the same colour as the pileus, but towards the apex generally darker and of a redder tinge.

---

* This mushroom, famous for the flavour it imparts to rich soups and gravies, is also used in the French "à la mode" beef shops in London, with the view of heightening the flavour of that dish. As the aroma is dissipated by overcooking, it should be thrown in only a few minutes before serving. The dried Champignon is much more extensively used in France and Italy than it is in England.

AG. OREADES.

In dense rings, or gregarious. Pileus smooth, *fleshy, convex, subumbonate*, generally more or less *compressed*, or *sinuate; tough*, coriaceous, *elastic, wrinkled*, when *water-soaked brown, buff* or *cream-colour* when dry; the umbo often remaining *red-brown*, as if *scorched*. Gills *distant*, ventricose, of the *same tint as the pileus* or *paler*. Stem equal, *solid, twisted*, very *tough* and *fibrous, pure, silky, white;* base downy, somewhat rooting and attached to the roots of grass.*

AG. SEMIGLOBATUS.

Pileus hemispherical, *viscid* when moist, *shining* and *smooth* as if varnished, obtuse, fleshy. Gills very broad, perfectly *horizontal to the stem*, broadly adnate, with a little tooth, minutely *serrated*, mottled with purple-brown sporules. *Stalk very viscid*, shining when dry with a closely-matted silkiness, *fistulose*, sometimes bulbous with a hollow bulb; ring generally complete, reflexed, often dusted with the dark-coloured spores.

AGARICUS NEBULARIS.

Plate IV. Fig. 2.

Subgenus Clitocybe.   Section Dasyphylli, *Fries*.

Ag. pileolarius, *Bulliard*.

"Il est très-agréable au goût."—*Bulliard*.

The following description was made from some among the more characteristic specimens of a large supply which I gathered this autumn (1847) near Hayes, from a spot where they are in the habit of re-appearing regularly in October.

Pileus from two and a half to five inches across; at first depresso-convex; when expanded nearly flat or broadly subumbonate, never depressed, margin at first involute and pruinose; occasionally somewhat waved and lobed, but generally

---

* Although the *Ag. oreades* be, properly speaking, a terrestrial and not a parasitical fungus, still as it springs up amidst the roots of the grasses and flourishes by depriving them of their supplies, the herbage in its neighbourhood is the first to scorch up and wither.

regular in form; smooth, viscid when moist, so that dead leaves adhere to it; grey, brown at the centre, paler towards the circumference. *Flesh* thick, white, unchanging; *gills* cream-colour, narrow, decurrent, close, their margins waved, unequal, generally simple. *Stem* from two to four inches long, from a quarter of an inch to an inch thick; incurved at the base, not rooting, but attaching by means of a floccose down, round its lower portion and for one-third of its length, a large quantity of dead leaves, by which the plant is held erect; subequal, more or less marked with longitudinal pits, firm externally, within of a softer substance. The *odour* strong, like that of curd cheese.

This Agaric appears to be local in Italy; otherwise it could scarcely have been omitted in Vittadini's work, nor by the author of the article "Fungo" in the Venice edition of the 'Dizionario Classico di Medicina:' add to which that I have never met with it myself either at Florence, Pisa, Naples, or Leghorn. That it grows in the neighbourhood of Rome is certain, since I find it admirably delineated in a curious collection of very old drawings which I purchased there. Moreover Professor Sanguinetti, of that city, writes in terms of high commendation of this mushroom, which, he says, may be discerned *inter alia*, " by its peculiar odour and grateful taste: when properly cooked it is equal to any of our funguses, rivalling not only the *Ag. prunulus*, but even the *Cæsareus:* as few are aware of its good qualities, it seldom finds its way into the Roman market." The *Ag. nebularis* requires but little cooking; a few minutes' broiling (à la Maintenon is best), with butter, pepper, and salt, is sufficient. It may also be delicately fried with bread crumbs, or stewed in white sauce. The flesh of this mushroom is perhaps lighter of digestion than that of any other.

CANTHARELLUS CIBARIUS.

Plate VIII. Fig. 1.

Tribe Mesopus.   Subdivision Agaricini, *Fries.*

"Sunt qui hunc perniciosum scripsere. Verum etiam latranti stomacho cum comedi; atque ex eo pulmenta parantur, quæ si aridis mortuorum oribus admoveantur percam ni reviviscerent!"—*Batt.*

"Jure inter sapidissimos fungos numeratur."—*Fries.*

No fungus is more popular than the above, though the merits—nay, the very existence—of such a fungus at home is confined to the Freemasons, who keep the secret! Having collected a quantity at Tunbridge Wells, this summer, and given them to the cook at the Calverley Hotel to dress, I learnt from the waiter that they were not novelties to him; that, in fact, he had been in the habit of dressing them for years, on state occasions, at the Freemasons' Tavern. They were generally fetched, so he said, from the neighbourhood of Chelmsford, and were always well paid for. Of the *Cantharellus*, this summer (1847), the supplies were immense! the moss under the beech-trees in Buckhurst Park in particular, was so lavish of them, that a hamper might soon have been filled, had there been hands to gather them. On revisiting the same park about five weeks later, they were still continuing to come up, but in less abundance.

The botanical characters of the *Cantharellus* are as follow:—

When young, its *stalk* is tough, white, and solid; but as it grows this becomes hollow and presently changes to yellow; tapering below, it is effused into the substance of the *pileus*, which is of the same colour with it. The *pileus* is lobed, and irregular in shape, its margin at first deeply involute, afterwards when expanded, wavy. The *veins* or plaits are thick, subdistant, much sinuated, running some way down the stalk.

The *flesh* is white, fibrous, dense, "having the odour of apricots" (*Purton*), or of "plums" (*Vitt.*). The *colour* yellow, that of the yolk of eggs, is deeper on the under surface; when raw it has the pungent taste of pepper; the *spores* which are elliptic, are of a pallid ochre colour (*Vitt.*).* The *Chantarelle* grows sometimes sporadically, sometimes in circles or segments of a circle, and may be found from June to October. At first it assumes the shape of a minute cone; next, in consequence of the rolling in of the margin, the pileus is almost spherical, but as this unfolds, it becomes hemispherical, then flat, at length irregular and depressed.

"This fungus," observes Vittadini, "being rather dry and tough by nature, requires a considerable quantity of fluid sauce to cook it properly." The common people in Italy dry or pickle, or keep it in oil for winter use. Perhaps the best ways of dressing the *Cantharellus* are to stew or mince it by itself, or to combine it with meat or with other funguses. It requires to be gently stewed and a long time to make it tender; but by soaking it in milk the night before, less cooking will be requisite.

The *Canth. cibarius* is very abundant about Rome, where it fetches, not being in great esteem, from twopence to twopence halfpenny a pound.

AGARICUS ATRAMENTARIUS, *Bull.*

Plate IX. Figs. 1 and 2.

Subgenus Coprinus, *Fries.*

Bot. Char. *Pileus* fleshy, campanulate, margin uneven,

* I have, however, found them *white*.

colour greyish, then light brown, slightly hairy, often corrugated, sometimes scaly in the centre. *Gills* numerous, deep, with clear veins, light brown, black in age, the edges grey or white, free, obtuse behind. *Stem* about four inches high, swollen at the base, piped, juicy, fibrous, marked with bands.

This is a common fungus in gardens, waste corners of fields, and lanes, and occasionally growing on stumps of trees in such situations: it is gregarious and cæspitose, and occurs both in spring and autumn. Young specimens afford a fine ketchup.

AGARICUS COMATUS.

Plate VII. Figs. 1, 2, and 3.

Subgenus Coprinus, *Fries*.

"A fungus in great request about Via Reggio and Lucca."—*Puccinelli*.

Bot. Char. *Pileus* cylindrical, breaking up into long scales, campanulate, epidermis thin, flesh thick in the centre, very thin and stringy at the margins. *Gills* numerous, quite free, leaving a space round the top of the stem. *Stem* from four to five inches high, rather bulbous at the base, stuffed with fibres, brittle, ring moveable.

This fungus may be found from early spring till late in the autumn, in meadows and waste places.

When used for making ketchup or for the table, only young specimens should be selected.

AGARICUS HETEROPHYLLUS, *Fries.*

Plate III. Figs. 3 and 4.

Subgenus Russula, *Scopoli.*

MILD RUSSULÆ. RUSSULÆ MITES, auct.

"Non meno sicuro e gustoso del Cesareo e del Porcino."—*Ttt.*

It is of the utmost importance that those who gather funguses for the table, should be accurately acquainted with the different species composing this genus; its members are so abundantly distributed; some of them form so excellent and delicate a food, whilst others produce such deleterious effects on the economy, that they are well entitled to a diligent and careful attention. The limits of this work will not permit an accurate discrimination of all the species, which would require a long monograph to themselves; but I have endeavoured to point out amidst those of most frequent occurrence, the three which may be selected with profit for the table, and some others which are nearly allied, from which we must be careful to separate them.

The three mild-flavoured *Russulæ* are the *Ag. heterophyllus, Ag. ruber,* and *Ag. virescens;* the botanical characters of the first are as follows:—

Ag. heterophyllus.

Pileus subirregular, from three and a half to four and a half inches across, at first convex, then more or less excavated towards the centre; for the most part smooth, the epidermis covering it, more or less moist, never scored or fissured, but exhibiting a continuous surface, marked by very small raised lines, radiating as from the centre, and frequently crossing so as to present a very minute finely reticulated meshwork, sometimes slightly zoned, adhering to the flesh of the *pileus*, which peels away with it in flakes resembling asbestos. It is very various in colour, being found of all shades of yellow, lilac, azure, green, and sometimes a mixture of these in different parts. The margin even, *i. e.* not striate, irregularly elevated and depressed. The *gills* are watery white, rather numerous and thick, ascending, tapering away at their stalk extremity, rather broader at the other, some simple but many of them forked at the base, in a few instances branched; the imperfect gills very few, irregular, occasionally broadly adhering to the side of a perfect gill; the *stalk* naked, variable as to length and size, equal or attenuated slightly at the base, white like spermaceti, externally rugulose, and meshed, like the pileus, with minute meandering lines, internally stuffed with a compact subfriable medullary substance, which, as the fungus grows old, breaks up here and there into sinuses which gradually coalesce, till at last the whole stem becomes hollow. The parenchyma is compact, but not thick, and does not change colour when cut. The spores white, round, and very abundant. The *taste* sweet and nutty. *Odour* none.

This excellent fungus, which Vittadini pronounces to be not surpassed for fineness of flavour by *Am. Cæsarea* or by *B. edulis*, with either of which it is equally wholesome, has been introduced by Roques into the houses of many of his friends in the environs of Paris, some of whom prefer it to *Ag. campestris:* an opinion shared by several of our own friends on this side the Channel. It grows in great abundance during the summer months generally, and this year nowhere more plentifully than under the Elm-trees in Kensington Gardens. There must be no delay in dressing it, otherwise insects, who are as fond of it as we are, appropriate it to their larvæ, which in a few hours will utterly consume it; the flesh, being very tender, requires but slight cooking.

Agaricus ruber, Schœffer. *Ag. griseus*, Persoon.

"L'Agarico Rosso è uno dei funghi più delicati e gustosi che si conoscono."—*Vitt.*

Bot. Char. Pileus rather fleshy, at first hemispherical, then obtusely convex, and, when fully expanded, more or less excavated towards the centre. The margins at first even, at length tuberculo-sulcate, that is, marked with lines similar to those left on the skin after cupping. The epidermis dry in dry weather, but very sticky in moist, of various hues, tawny-purple, olive-green, ochraceous-yellow, or several of these united, and generally darkest at the centre; peeling off readily without laceration of the flesh. The flesh white, when cut slightly rufescent, when dry cream-coloured. The *gills* fragile, cream-coloured, connected below by transverse plaits or veins, thick and broad, but tapering away towards the stalk, really simple, though a few imperfect gills interposed between the entire ones, and attaching themselves to their sides give these sometimes the appearance of being forked; the *stalk* equal, white, or blotched here and there with purple stains, stuffed, brittle, and Vittadini adds, "long," which is not my experience of it; when young it is so short as to be entirely hid by the globose head of the unexpanded pileus. The flesh inconsiderable but compact; *sporules* pale-buff.

The *Ag. ruber*, the *Colomba rossa* of the Tuscans, and *Rother Täubling* of Schœffer, is a complete *wood*-pigeon in its haunts; it grows very abundantly, may be gathered from July to a very late period in the autumn, and is as delicate and light of digestion as the *Russula* last described. It may be readily distinguished from *Ag. alutaceus* by the different colour of its gills and spores, which in that species are buff, but in the *Ag. ruber* cream-coloured: moreover the greater thickness of the substance of the pileus of *Ag. alutaceus*, the margin of which is deeply sulcate, even at an early period of its development, and the pungent acrid taste, which is seldom wanting, are further means of distinguishing it from *Ag. ruber*. *Ag. emeticus* differs from it in having unequal snow-white gills, and in extreme acrimony of taste.

Agaricus virescens, Schœff.: the Verdette? *Ag. bifidus*, Bull.
Russula æruginosa, Persoon.

" La carne di questo Agarico è tenera e di sapore gratissimo."—*Vitt*.

Pileus at first flatly convex; at length depressed towards the centre with an even margin; epidermis whitish, fibrous, continuous and firmly adhering to the flesh, dry, but coated over with a thick stratum of opaque meal, which gradually breaking as the pileus expands maps it in a singular and quite characteristic manner with a series of irregular polygonal figures, in greater or less relief according to the thickness of the coating; its colour varies slightly but is generally made up of some admixture of green and yellow, communicating to the surface, as Bulliard has remarked, a farinaceous or mouldy appearance. The *gills* of some thickness, very brittle, white, sublanceolate, generally simple, but occasionally forked, the imperfect gills interspersed without order amongst the entire ones; the *stalk* equal, short, its centre stuffed with cottony fibres: somewhat compact and elastic. According to Thore, as quoted by Persoon, this Agaric may be cultivated.*

* " Dans le département des Landes on sème l'Agaricus Palomet. Pour cela on se contente d'arroser la terre d'un bosquet planté en chênes avec de l'eau dans laquelle on a fait bouillir une grande quantité de ces champignons; la culture n'exige d'autres soins que d'éloigner de ces lieux les chevaux, les porcs et les bêtes à cornes, qui sont très-friandes de ces plantes; ce moyen réussit toujours, mais nous laissons aux physiciens à nous expliquer pourquoi l'ébullition n'a pas fait mourir les germes."—*Thore*.

It is an exceedingly delicate fungus, but not very common in England. The best way of cooking it, according to Vittadini, is on the gridiron; the peasants about Milan are in the habit of putting it over wood embers to toast, eating it afterwards with a little salt, in which way it has a savoury smell, and a taste like that of the *Cancer astacus*; when fresh it is without odour, but acquires a very strong one while drying, which he compares to that of salt meat. Mr. Berkeley quotes Roques' authority as to its being eaten in France; Vittadini, without giving any authority, states that it is eaten in England. It loses but little of its volume in drying.

ACRID RUSSULÆ. RUSSULÆ ACRES, Auct.

Agaricus alutaceus, Persoon.

Three acrid *Russulæ* remain to be described, *Ag. alutaceus*, *Ag. emeticus*, *Ag. sanguineus*; all three common, though not perhaps so common as the mild ones, and all to be avoided. The first, *A. alutaceus*, Fries, is ranked by Vittadini among the safe kinds, he even affixes a misplaced note of admiration after his epithet "esculentus!" and describes it even when raw as "a dainty food, possessed of a most agreeable flavour."

Mr. Berkeley, who reports it esculent when *young*, remarks that individual specimens occur, which prove almost as acrid as the *Ag. emeticus* itself; my own experience of it in England is, that whether young or old, it is always acrid when raw.*
I have never tried it dressed, which might possibly extract

---

* The reader must not conclude from this that soil, any more than age, will account for such differences; there is a *variety* of *Ag. alutaceus*, described by Vittadini, which he says is "endowed with a very caustic taste, smelling of pepper, and to be avoided." The kind *generally* found in England is probably the same as this, which Bulliard has described under the name of *Ag. alutaceus acris*.

its noxious qualities, as Vittadini reports to have been the case with a caustic variety which he subjected to this test; but since even then, on his own showing, it proved indigestible, I would advise no one to try this species, especially when there are so many others, the good qualities of which are known.

It is easy to distinguish *A. alutaceus* from any of the foregoing species; to do this it is only necessary to look at the gills, which, in place of being, as in these, white, watery white, or cream-coloured, are of a rich buff; *pileus* about three inches broad, pink or livid olive, smooth on the surface, and viscid in wet weather; the margin at first even, but in age striate; the *gills* broad, equal, slightly forked, ventricose, free, connected by veins; the *sporules* rich buff; the *stem* one and a half inches long, blunt, surface longitudinally wrinkled or grooved, solid without, spongy within, varying from white to buff.

Agaricus emeticus, Schœffer.

Reports concerning the qualities of this fungus differ widely, some asserting it to be a most deleterious species, of which the mischief was not to be removed by cooking, whilst others, on the authority of dogs whom they persuaded to eat some, pronounced it innoxious. In this state of uncertainty Vittadini, for the sake of science, and peradventure of adventure also, determined to test its effects upon himself; he had previously given at different times large doses, of from six to twelve ounces, to dogs, both in the crude state and also cooked; but without result. " Still," says he,[*] " thinking that though dogs might eat *Ag. emeticus* with impunity, it might yet

---

[*] "Sospettando ragionevolmente dietro le esperienze del Krapf e del Roques che questo fungo potesse esser nocivo all' uomo e non agli animali, ho voluto anch' io sperimentarlo su di me stesso."—*Vitt.*

prove injurious to man, I took five specimens of fair dimensions, and having fried, I ate them with the usual condiments; but though pains were taken to have them delicately prepared (*ottimamente cucinati*), they still retained their acrid bitter taste, and were most distasteful to the palate." The reader will be glad to learn, that the only inconvenience suffered by this bold self-experimentalist was a slight sense of præcordial uneasiness accompanied with flatulence,—effects attributable entirely, as he believed, to the rich mode in which his dish was prepared: though, more timid apparently for others' safety than his own, he particularly adds, "though I have clearly established to my own satisfaction, the complete innocuousness of the *A. emeticus*: still, as there are, or are said to be, other *Russulæ* of highly deleterious properties and closely allied, the mistaking which for it might be paid for by the loss of life, the safer rule is to abstain from all such as have acrid juices."

The botanical characters of *Ag. emeticus* are as follow:—

Pileus more or less rosy, flesh compact, margin striate, epidermis adherent; *gills* very brittle, arched in front, attenuated towards the stalk, connected below by transverse plaits, generally simple, a few forked, the imperfect gills rounded off behind; the *stalk*, which is compact, of equal dimensions, and white, is generally more or less stained with red spots of the same hue as the pileus; in the growing fungus, where the epidermis has been removed and the flesh eaten by insects, this soon acquires a tint as lively as that of the skin itself; generally I have remarked that the erosions of insects and slugs do *not* produce any change of colour, even in the species notorious under other circumstances for manifesting such a change; thus the flesh of the *Ag. rubescens*, which turns red when it is divided, may be frequently seen half eaten through, exhibiting a white flesh; and the same is the case with the *Boletus luridus*, the flesh of which, though eroded, remains white till it is broken through.

Ag. sanguineus, Bull.

This fungus, of which the general facies and most of the botanical characters, as well as the taste and other qualities, are similar to those of the last-mentioned Agaric, differs from it in having its gills for the most part forked, many smaller ones being interposed between those that are entire, also in *not* having its margin striate, as the *Ag. emeticus* when moderately expanded always has. The smell of this fungus, which is only developed in drying, is, according to Vittadini, "most agreeable," resembling that of fresh meal; to me its odour is unpleasant and like that of sour paste.

Ag. acris minor.

Pileus one or two inches across, sticky, of a light muddy-pink, the *epidermis* peeling off easily and entire from the flesh, margin not striate, flesh soft, white, and cellular; *gills* adnate, white, forked, brittle, slightly ventricose; the margin sub-denticulate; the *stalk* of spermaceti-whiteness and appearance, solid within, brittle, the internal texture looser than the external; the surface minutely rugulose, $1\frac{1}{4}$–$1\frac{1}{2}$ inch, by 2–4 lines thick, intensely acrid. In meadows, throughout the summer; abundant.

AGARICUS OSTREATUS, *Jacq.*
Plate X.

Subgenus Pleuropus, *Persoon.*   Subdivision Concharia, *Fries.*

> "L'Ag. ostreato viene giustamente per la sua bontà ed innocenza amesso tra i funghi commestibili, de' quali è pure permessa la vendita sulle pubbliche piazze."—*Vitt.*

Bot. Char. Cæspitose.* *Pileus* fleshy, smooth, blackish, then cinereous, at length paler; epidermis strongly adherent, flesh fibrous, moderately firm; *gills* anastomosing behind, not glandular, white; *stem* sublateral or wanting. On dead trees.† Season, spring and autumn.

As there are some singular differences presented by this fungus in regard to development, odour, taste, and the colour of the spores, which seem almost sufficient to entitle it to be divided into two distinct species, I shall first describe the more ordinary form, as given by Mr. Berkeley, and then mention the variations from it.

"Imbricated, large; *pileus* subdimidiate, very thick and fleshy; flesh white, dusky towards the surface; one inch deep, the border at first fibrillose; margin involute, as the pileus expands the white fibrillæ vanish, and the colour changes to bistre; margin paler and rimulose, the whole surface shining and satiny when dry, soft and clammy when moist; *gills* broad, here and there forked,"‡ standing out sharp and erect like the fine flutings of a column, winding down the stalk to different lengths, and those that reach the bottom forming there a beautiful raised meshwork highly characteris-

---
* I lately found a *single* specimen of it, which Vittadini says is rare.
† On the Poplar and Willow, according to Vittadini; Apple and Laburnum, on the authority of Berkeley; Elm and Ash, on my own.
‡ In some specimens the gills are *all* solitary.

tic of this species, "*dirty* (pure?) white, the edge serrated, umber; *taste* and *smell* like that of *Ag. personatus*, which it resembles somewhat in colour;" "*spores* white like those of the *Polyporus suaveolens*."* The points of difference in those which departed from the ordinary type were as follows :†—first, in specimens growing close together and all equally exposed to the light, the colour of all at the same period of growth was not the same, being a delicate waxy-white in some of the specimens, in others, a light-brown. Secondly, whereas this fungus is generally "invested during infancy with a *white lanugo or down*,"‡ I observed the young Agarics, which presented themselves at first as small semitransparent eminences rising irregularly from a common stalk, and not unlike in appearance the blisters on a chalcedony, to be thickly coated with a light-blue varnish in place of it; the dry *débris* of which varnish continued to adhere to the surface of the pileus for some time afterwards. Thirdly, the complexion of the spores, commonly described as *white*, was in these specimens pale-rose. Fourthly, they exhaled the strong and peculiar odour of Tarragon; and, finally, in place of being the delicate fungus at table which in July I had always found it, these specimens afforded a distasteful food. The *Ag. ostreatus* resists cold in a remarkable manner; the circumstance of its being found in winter has procured for it the trivial name of Gelon. *Ag. ostreatus* is found on the barks of many sorts of trees, and wherever it has once been it is apt to recur frequently afterwards. It may be dressed in any of the more usual ways; but as the flesh is rather over-solid and tenacious, it is all the better for being cooked leisurely over a slow fire.

* Vitt.

† It is probable that the varieties here referred to belonged to *Ag. enosmus*, B. Care must be taken to distinguish between the two, as *Ag. enosmus* is an unsafe species.—ED. ‡ Vitt.

AGARICUS RUBESCENS, *Persoon*.

Plate XI. Figs. 3, 4, and 5.

Subgenus 1. Amanita.

"Non altrimenti del Cesareo delicato e sano."—*Vitt.*

Bot. Char. Pileus covered with warts of different sizes; margins even, convex, flesh turns obscurely red when cut or bruised, slightly moist and shining; *gills* attenuated behind; *stem* at first stuffed, in age becoming hollow, bulbous, sometimes scaly; *ring* wide, marked with striæ; *spores* nearly elliptical; *smell* strong; *taste* not unpleasant.

This is a very delicate fungus, which grows in sufficient abundance to render it of importance in a culinary point of view. It makes excellent ketchup. Cordier reports it as one of the most delicate mushrooms of the Lorraine; and Roques speaks equally well of it. It generally grows in woods, particularly of oak and chestnut, both in summer and autumn. No fungus is more preyed upon than this by mice, snails, and insects.

MORCHELLA ESCULENTA, *Dill.*

Plate XII. Figs. 6 and 7.

Tribe 3. Mitrati.

Morell.

"Sommamente ricercata."—*Vitt.*

Every one knows the Morell, that expensive luxury which the rich are content to procure at great cost from our Italian warehouses, and the poor are fain to do without. It is less generally known that this fungus, though by no means so common with us as some others, (a circumstance partly attributable to the prevailing ignorance as to when and where to look for it, or even of its being indigenous to England,*) occurs not unfrequently in our orchards and woods, towards the beginning of summer. Roques reports favourably of some specimens sent to him by the Duke of Athol; and others, from different parts of the country, occasionally find their way into Covent Garden market. The genus *Morchella* comprises very few species, and they are all good to eat. Persoon remarks, that though the Morell rarely appears in a sandy soil, preferring a calcareous or argillaceous ground, it frequently springs up on sites where charcoal has been burnt or where cinders have been thrown.

Morchella esculenta.

Bot. Char. Pileus very various in shape and hue, the surface broken up into little sinuses or cells, made by folds or plaits of the hymenium, which are more or less salient, and constitute the so-called ribs. These *ribs* are very irregular, and anastomose with each other throughout; the pileus hollow, opening into the irregular hollow stem. *Spores* pale-yellow.

Morchella semilibera.

Bot. Char. This may be known from the *M. esculenta* by being, as its name imports, half free, *i. e.* having the pileus for half its length detached from the stalk. Spores are pale-

---

* A countryman, last spring (1817), stumbled upon a large quantity in the neighbourhood of Chiselhurst, Kent, and being struck with their appearance gathered some, and took them to a medical man of the place, who, not recognizing the plant, suffered the whole to perish! He has since been made aware of his mistake.

yellow. Odour, at first feeble, becomes stronger in drying. Occurring less frequently than the last, and much less sapid. Neither of these funguses should be gathered after rain, as they are then insipid and soon spoil.*

M. Roques says the Morell may be dressed in a variety of ways, both fresh and dry, with butter or in oil, *au gras* or *à la créme*. The following receipts for cooking them are from Persoon.

1st. Having washed and cleansed them from the earth which is apt to collect between the plaits, dry thoroughly in a napkin, and put them into a saucepan with pepper, salt, and parsley, adding or not a piece of ham; stew for an hour, pouring in occasionally a little broth to prevent burning; when sufficiently done, bind with the yolks of two or three eggs, and serve on buttered toast.

2nd. *Morelles à l'Italienne.*—Having washed and dried, divide them across, put them on the fire with some parsley, scallion, chervil, burnet, tarragon, chives, a little salt, and two spoonfuls of fine oil. Stew till the juice runs out; then thicken with a little flour; serve with bread-crumbs and a squeeze of lemon.

3rd. *Stuffed Morells.*—Choose the freshest and whitest Morells, open the stalk at the bottom; wash and wipe them well, fill with veal stuffing, anchovy, or any rich *farce* you please, securing the ends, and dressing between thin slices of bacon. Serve with a sauce like the last.†

---

* It is a common fraud in the Italian market for the salesmen to soak them in water; which increases their weight, but spoils their flavour.

† In the Roman market the Morell is held in little esteem, and sells for 4d. or 5d. per lb. Three varieties of the *esculenta* are brought in by the "Asparagarii," *i.e.* the peasants who gather the *wild* Asparagus on the hills; viz. the *M. rotunda*, which is almost globose, *M. vulgaris*, and *M. fulva*, which is of a tawny colour.

HYDNUM REPANDUM, *Linn.*
Plate VIII. Figs. 3 and 4.
Subgenus Mesopus, *Fries.*

"The general use made of this fungus throughout France, Italy, and Germany leaves no doubt as to its good qualities."—*Roques.*

Bot. Char. Pileus fleshy, tawny, red, smoothly tomentose, very irregular in shape, from two to five inches across, lobed or undulated; margin vaulted, acute, wavy; flesh white, turning yellow when cut, if bruised becoming brown-red; *spines* pale-yellow, unequal, thick-set, apices canino-denticulate or conical, straight or slightly ungulate; occasionally bifid; shorter and more obtuse towards the stalk, on the upper part of which they are somewhat decurrent, leaving small foraminules when detached; *stem* at first white, then tawny; two inches long, solid, of variable thickness (from half an inch to two inches) more or less flattened, papillated above with the rudiments of spines which have aborted; *spores* round, white, *taste* when raw at first pleasant, but presently of a saline bitter, like Glauber salts, somewhat peppery, and *smell* like that of horse-radish.

This fungus occurs principally in woods, and especially in those of pine and oak; sometimes solitary, but more frequently in company and in rings. In Italy (where the spines have procured for it the name of "Steccherino," or Hedgehog), it is brought into the market and sold promiscuously with the Chantarelle, to which in colour and in some other respects it bears a resemblance. There is no fungus with which this is likely to be confounded; once seen, it is recognized at a glance afterwards, and may be gathered fearlessly.

According to Paulet, Persoon, and Vittadini, the *Hyd. re-*

pandum should be cooked for a long time, and with plenty of sauce, otherwise, being deficient in moisture, it is apt to become rather tough; when well stewed it is an excellent dish, with a slight flavour of oysters; it makes also a very good *purée*. Vittadini places it among the most delicate of the funguses of Italy.

FISTULINA HEPATICA, *Fries*.
Plate XII. Figs. 1 and 2.

"Fungus pauperibus esculentus."—*Schæff*.

This fungus, which, in the earlier stages of its development, frequently resembles very closely a tongue in shape, structure, and general appearance, presents later a dark, amorphous, grumous-looking mass, bearing a still more striking likeness to liver. Thus, seen while young, and just beginning to bud out from the oak,* its papillated surface, regular shape, and clear fibrous flesh make it an object of interest to many who, introduced to it at an advanced period of growth, can hardly be brought to believe that the blackened misshapen mass, that looks like liver, and that deeply stains the fingers with an unsightly red fluid, can indeed be the same plant. It has, from the earliest-recorded accounts, been designated by names pointing to these resemblances: Cesalpinus calls it *Linguæ*; Wallemb, *Buglossus quercinus*; the vulgar name in Italy is "Lingua quercina," or "Lingua di castagna." It constitutes a genus by itself.

* Though the *F. hepatica* grows both upon oak and chestnut trees, this difference in its origin never perceptibly affects the plant, which is equally good, whether it be gathered from one or from the other.

Bot. Char. Pileus confluent with the stalk: at first studded on the upper side with minute papillæ (the rudiments of tubes), which afterwards disappear; flesh succulent, fibrous, like beet-root in appearance, with a vinous smell and a slight acid taste; *tubes* continuous with the fibres of the receptacle, unequal, very short, small, cylindrical, ochraceous-rufescent; at first with closed pores, but as they elongate they become patent; colour at first a dry dusky white, afterwards a yellowish-red; the whole surface more or less sticky, with a gelatinous secretion exuding from it; *sporidia* ochraceous-green, and matured at different times from the unequal length of the tubes. This fungus varies in size from that of a small kidney to an irregular mass of many pounds' weight, and of several feet in circumference. I recently picked a specimen which measured nearly five feet round, and weighed upwards of eight pounds; but this is nothing to one found by Mr. Graves, which, on the authority of Mr. Berkeley, weighed nearly thirty pounds.

The *Fistulina hepatica*, which Schœffer calls the Poor Man's fungus, "fungus pauperibus esculentus," deserves indeed the epithet if we look to its abundance, which makes it an acquisition to the labouring class wherever it is known; but that it is in any other sense fitted for the poor, or to be eaten by those only who can purchase no other food, is what I cannot subscribe to. No fungus yields a richer gravy, and though rather tough, when grilled it is scarcely to be distinguished from broiled meat. The best way to dress it if old, is to stew it down for stock, and reject the flesh, but if young, it may be eaten in substance, plain, or with minced meat; in all cases its succulency is such that it furnishes its own sauce, which a friend of ours, well versed in the science of the table, declares each time he eats it to be "undeniably good."

In England the *F. hepatica* grows principally on old oak-trees, and may be found throughout the summer in great abundance.

AGARICUS ORCELLA,* *Bull.*
Plate XI. Figs. 1 and 2.
Section Mouceron, *Fries.*

"Senza dubbio uno de' migliori funghi indigeni."—*Vitt.*
"Esculentus!"—*Ibid.*

This is a very delicate mushroom; it grows either solitary or in company, and sometimes in rings, succeeding occasionally a crop of *Ag. oreades* and *Ag. prunulus* which had recently occupied the same site. Its general appearance, once recognized, is such as to render the mistaking it for any other species afterwards unlikely, whilst the least attention to its botanical characters makes it impossible to do so. Its irregular lobed pileus with smooth undulated borders, its decurrent gills, and short solid stem are so many particulars in which at first it might seem to resemble in outline the *Canth. cib.*, with which it has, however, nothing else in common. It bears a nearer general resemblance to several of the section *Lactifluus* of Persoon, but the exudation, or not, of milk would be conclusive in any doubtful case, to say nothing of its peculiar smell of cucumber rind, or syringa leaf,† in which respect it resembles no other fungus. The surface is as soft and smooth to the touch as kid, except in wet weather, when

---

* Whence the vernacular names, "Orgella," "Orgelle," and "Oreille."
† Most authors compare this odour to that of fresh meal, but as several friends think with me that the above comparison is more accurate, I have ventured to substitute it.

it becomes more or less sticky; the size, which does not admit of much variation, is from two to three inches across; whilst young the borders are rolled inwards towards the gills, the stalk is in the centre, and somewhat enlarged at the base; but as the fungus grows the borders unroll themselves, one side grows more rapidly than the other, the stalk becomes, in consequence, eccentric, and this eccentricity is often rendered greater by a lateral twist towards the base. The gills, which at first are white, assume later a pale salmon hue; Berkeley adds that "they are more or less forked, covered with very minute conical papillæ ending in four spiculæ;" those that are entire taper away posteriorly and terminate on the stalk, but the imperfect ones are rounded off midway; the spores are elliptic, and of the colour of brown-holland.*

This mushroom is found occasionally, throughout the summer, but autumn is the season to look for it, amidst the grass of woods and pastures, where it abounds. It should be eaten the day it is gathered, either stewed, broiled, or fried with egg and bread-crumbs, like cutlets. When dried, it loses much of its volume and acquires "a very sweet smell,"—"un' aroma suavissimo" (*Vitt.*).

HELVELLA CRISPA, *Fries*.
HELVELLA LACUNOSA, *Afz*.
Tribe MITRATI, *Fries*.

"Può essere con vantaggio raccolta ed agli stessi usi delle spugniole destinata."—*Vitt.*

All *Helvellæ* are esculent, have an agreeable odour, and bear

---

* Mr. Berkeley says rose-coloured; Vittadini pale rust-colour; but I find that on placing a watchglass thickly coated with spores on fine brown-holland, the colours very nearly correspond.

a general resemblance in flavour to the *Morell*. The *Helvella crispa*, or pallid Helvella of Scopoli and Fries, is, it seems, " not uncommon,"* and the *Helvella lacunosa*, or cinereous Helvella of Afzel (on each of whose heads respectively Sowerby and Schœffer place an *inappropriate* mitre), are both indigenous. They are thus succinctly but excellently described by Mr. Berkeley.

Helvella crispa, Fries.

Bot. Char. *Pileus* whitish, flesh-coloured or yellowish, deflexed, lobed, free, crisped, pallid; *stem* fistulose, costato-lacunose, 3–5 inches high, snowy-white, deeply lacunose and ribbed, the *ribs* hollow.

Helvella lacunosa, Afzel.

Bot. Char. *Pileus* inflated, lobed, cinereous,† lobes deflexed, adnate, stem fistulose, costato-lacunose; *stem* white or dusky.

This *Helvella* is not so common as the last, neither is it so sapid. They both grow in woods and on the stumps of old trees. Bendiscioli places them, for flavour, before the *Morell*, but this is not the general opinion entertained of them.

Helvella esculenta, Pers.

PLATE XII. FIGS. 3, 4, AND 5.

Bot. Char. *Pileus* inflated, irregular, undulated, gyrosorugose, of a rich dark-brown colour, margin united with the

---

* Berk. Brit. Fung.

† The lobes are at first nearly white, afterwards of an ash-grey colour on the under surface; the upper, or that which bears the seed membrane, continuing white.

stem; *stem* white or dusky. In plantations of fir and chestnut adjoining Weybridge Heath, in Surrey. It has not yet been found elsewhere in Britain.

VERPA DIGITALIFORMIS, *Persoon*.
PEZIZA ACETABULUM, *Linn*.

Tribe CUPULATI.

These funguses are very similar in their properties to the *Helvellæ*; that is, are not to be despised when one cannot get better, nor to be eaten when one can. "The *Verpa*," says Vittadini, "though sold in the market, is only to be recommended when no other esculent fungus offers, which is sometimes the case in spring." The *Peziza acetabulum* is utterly insipid, and depends entirely for flavour upon the sauce in which it is served. As they are rare in England, I shall merely give the botanical character of each.

Verpa digitaliformis, Persoon.

Pileus campanulate, three-quarters of an inch high, more or less closely pressed to the stem, but always free, wrinkled, but not reticulated, under side slightly pubescent, *sporidia* yellowish, elliptic, *stem* three inches high, half an inch thick, equal or slightly attenuated downwards, loosely stuffed, by no means hollow, transversely squamulose.* Season, spring.

* Another species of *Peziza*, the *P. cochleata*, grew very abundantly last spring in Holwood Park, Keston. This species is quite insipid, and somewhat leathery, but Mr. Berkeley has seen it offered for sale under the name of Morell.

Peziza acetabulum, Linn. Series *Aleuria*, Section *Helvella*, Fries.

Bot. Char. Deeply cup-shaped, two inches broad, one and a half deep, externally floccose, light-umber, darker within, mouth puckered, tough; *stem* half to one inch high, smooth, deeply but irregularly costato-lacunose, ribs solid "branching at the top and forming reticulations on the outside of the cup, so as to present the appearance of a cluster of pillars supporting a font or roof, with fret-work between them" (*Berkeley*). Season, spring.

POLYPORUS FRONDOSUS, *Schrank*.
PLATE IV. FIG. 1.

There are many species of *Polyporus* eaten on the Continent; among the more common kinds to be mentioned are *P. frondosus* and *P. tuberaster*, Persoon, *P. corylinus*, Mauri, *P. subsquamosus*, Pers., *P. giganteus*, ibid., *P. fomentarius*, ibid., which last is the Amadou, or German tinder fungus. Two of these are local; the *P. tuberaster*, which occurs principally in the kingdom of Naples, and the *P. corylinus* or that of the cob-nut tree, which (though it might perhaps be cultivated elsewhere) is at present restricted to Rome; both these are excellent for food.

As to the *Polyporus squamosus*, which is as common in England as abroad, in substance it cannot be masticated, and its expressed juice is exceedingly disagreeable; I should not think the *P. fomentarius*, to judge from its texture, promised much better; nor *P. giganteus*, of which the flesh is sometimes so tough as to creak under the knife.

The true *P. frondosus* is probably rare in England, that which I have met with and have had cooked, without being able to say much in its favour, is the *P. intybaceus* of Fries, which Mr. Berkeley says is distinguished from the other by having larger pores. Vittadini has not included it among the esculent funguses in his work; Persoon does not recommend it for weak stomachs on account of its toughness.* Paulet, indeed, is of a different opinion, telling us that in place of its being heavy for the stomach, *he* will feel all the lighter who sups upon it. The people in the Vosges seem to have an equal affection for it with this writer, giving it the somewhat whimsical, though really most graphic *sobriquets* of the Hen-of-the-Woods and the Breeding Hen (Mougeot). Professor Sanguinetti informs me that it sells for six or seven baiocchi in the Roman market, the finer specimens being sent as surprise presents, "per meraviglia," from poor tenants to hard landlords.

Bot. Char. "*Pilei* very numerous, dimidiate, condensed into a convex tuft from half a foot to a foot broad, imbricated, variously confluent, irregular, at first downy, dusky, then smooth, livid grey; disk depressed, dilated above, from half to one inch broad, convex, the base confluent with the compound stem " (*Fries*).

* The toughness is owing to its being stewed too quickly; when properly sweated with butter, as recommended for *C. coralloides*, it is quite tender.

CLAVARIA CORALLOIDES, *Linn.*

PLATE V. FIG. 3.

Subgenus OCHROSPOREA, *Fries.*

"Esculenta deliciosa."—*Vitt.*

All the funguses of this genus being esculent, enter more or less largely into the supplies of the Italian markets. Roques describes seven species; Persoon five; Vittadini gives a detailed account and drawings of three, selecting those principally for the superiority of their flavour over the rest, and because of their greater abundance in the Milanese district. Mr. Berkeley, in a list with which he has favoured me, enumerates four British species as esculent, *C. coralloides*, *C. grisea*, *C. cristata*, and *C. rugosa*; as, however, he has no personal experience of any of these as articles of food, I shall merely give the botanical character of the *C. coralloides*, the most abundant of all the species (for the excellent qualities of which I can myself vouch), furnishing the reader with one or two drawings of other sorts, in further illustration of this elegant genus.

Clavaria coralloides.

Bot. Char. Pileus erect, white; *stem* rather thick, branches unequal, elongated, mostly acute, pure white, sometimes violet at the base.

Mode of Dressing.

Having thoroughly cleansed away the earth, which is apt to adhere to them, they are to be sweated with a little butter, over a slow fire, afterwards to be strained, then (throwing away the liquor) to be replaced to stew for an hour, with salt, pepper, chopped chives and parsley, moistening with plain stock, and dredging with flour occasionally. When sufficiently cooked, to be thickened with yolks of eggs and cream.

Another Mode.

Proceed as before; after sweating the *Clavarias*, wrap them in bacon and stew in a little broth seasoned with salt, pepper, parsley, and ham; cook for an hour, then serve in white sauce, or with a *fricassée* of chicken.

N.B.—The saucepan should be covered with a sheet of paper under the lid, which keeps the *Clavarias* white and also preserves their flavour.

There can be little doubt that our woods, properly explored, would be found to abound in funguses hitherto considered rare, and this would probably be one of them. At present the weald of Kent, within forty miles of London, remains, so far as Mycology is concerned, nearly as unexplored as the interior of Africa.

Plate V. fig. 2, represents *Clavaria amethystina*, Bull. Plate V. fig. 5, represents *C. cinerea*, Bull. Plate V., fig. 6, represents *C. rugosa*, Bull.

LYCOPERDON PLUMBEUM, *nob.*

Puff-balls.

Subdivision GASTEROMYCETES, *Fries.*

Tribe 3. TRICHOSPERMI.

Family 1. TRICHOGASTRES. GENUS 1. LYCOPERDON, *Tournef.*

"Il Licoperdo piombino è uno dei funghi mangiativi più delicati che si conoscano. Il suo uso è pressochè generale."—*Vitt.*

All these more or less spherical white funguses furnished

with a membranaceous covering, and filled when young with a white, compact, homogeneous pulp, which we call Puff-balls, are good to eat; those in most request for the table abroad, and the best, have no stem, *i. e.* no sterile base, but are prolific throughout their whole substance. One of the most common of these is the *Lycoperdon plumbeum,* of which the following excellent description is chiefly taken from Vittadini.

Bot. Char. Body globose; when full-grown about the size of a walnut, invested with two* tunics, the outer one white, loosely membranaceous and fragile, sometimes smooth, at others furfuraceous; the innermost one (peridium) very tenacious, smooth, of a grey-lead colour externally, internally more or less shaggy with very fine hairs; these hairs occupy the whole cavity, and in the midst of them a prodigious number of minute granular bodies, the sporules (each of which is furnished with a long caudiform process), lie entangled. The whole plant, carefully removed from the earth, with its root still adhering, is in form not unlike one of its own seeds vastly magnified.

The *L. plumbeum* abounds in dry places, and is to be found in spring, summer, and autumn, solitary or in groups. "This," says Vittadini, "is one of our commonest Puff-balls, and after the warm rains of summer and of autumn, myriads of these little plants suddenly springing up will often completely cover a piece of ground as if they had been sown like grain, for a crop; if we dig them up we shall find that they are connected with long fragile threads, extending horizontally underground and giving attachment to numerous smaller Puff-balls in dif-

---

* There are, in fact, three at first, whereof the external one either coalesces with the second, or else peels off in shreds, when the other two become united, and continue to maintain the globular form of the Puff-ball unimpaired, even after the escape of the seed.

ferent stages of development, which, by continuing to grow, afford fresh supplies as the old ones die off."

LYCOPERDON BOVISTA, *Linn.*

Subdivision GASTEROMYCETES, *Fries.*

Tribe 3. TRICHOSPERMI.   Family 1. TRICHOGASTRES.

"Vescie buone da friggere" (Tuscan vernacular name).

"La sua carne candida compatta si presta facilemente a tutte le speculazioni del cuoco."—*Vitt.*

This differs from the last-mentioned Puff-ball in many particulars; in the first place it is much larger (sometimes attaining to vast dimensions), its shape is different, being that of an inverted cone; never globular, the flesh also is more compact, while the membrane which holds what is first the pulp and afterwards the seed, is very thin and tender; the seed, moreover, has no caudal appendage; and finally, a considerable portion of the base is sterile, in all which additional particulars it is unlike the *Lycoperdon plumbeum.* The plant is sessile, a purple-black fragile membrane contains the spores, which are also sessile,* and of the same colour as the peridium.

No fungus requires to be eaten so soon after gathering as this; a few hours will destroy the compactness of the flesh and change its colour from delicate-white to dirty-yellow;†

---

* Without appendages.

† Vittadini recommends, wherever this fungus grows conveniently for the purpose, that it should not be all taken at once, but by slices cut off from the living plant, care being taken not to break up its attachments with the earth; in this way, he says, you may have a fine "frittura" every day for a week.

but when perfectly fresh and properly prepared, it yields to no other in digestibility. It may be dressed in many ways, but the best method is to cut it into slices and fry these in egg and bread-crumbs; so prepared, it has the flavour of a rich, light omelette.*

AGARICUS MELLEUS.
Plate IX. Fig. 3.
Subgenus 3. Amillaria.

This is a nauseous, disagreeable fungus, however cooked, and merely finds mention here, as its omission in a work on the esculent funguses of England might seem strange to those unacquainted with is demerits; it is really extraordinary how some Continental writers, speaking from their own experience, should ever have recommended it for the table. Pliny's general *apage* against all funguses really finds an application to this, which is so repugnant to our notions of the savoury, that few would make a second attempt, or get dangerously far in a first dish. Not to be poisonous is its only recommendation; for as to the inviting epithet *melleus*, or honeyed, by which it is designated, this alludes only to the colour, and by no means to the taste, which is both harsh and styptic.

Bot. Char. In tufts, near or upon stumps of trees, or posts. *Pileus* dirty-yellow, more or less hairy; *stem* fibrous, varying greatly in length, from one inch to nine or ten; enlarged above and below, thinner in the middle; *ring* thick, spread-

---

* I have been informed that this Puff-ball is sometimes served on state occasions at the Freemasons' Tavern.

ing, rough or leathery; *gills* somewhat decurrent, deeper than the pileus; *spores* white, appearing like fine dust on the gills.

AGARICUS ULMARIUS, *Bull.*

Subgenus PLEUROPUS. Subdivision ÆGERITARIA.

"Fungo mangiativo sommamente ricercato e di ottima qualità."—*Vitt.*

Bot. Char. Solitary or connected to others by a common root; the *pileus* presenting a dirty-white surface, turning afterwards to a pale rust-colour, and sometimes tessellated; varying like all parasitical funguses in shape, but generally more or less orbicular; flesh continuous with the stalk, white, compact; *stalk* very thick, solid, elastic, smooth towards the summit, tomentose at the base; *gills* of a yellowish tint, broad, thick, ventricose, emarginate, *i.e.* terminating upon the surface of the stem in a receding angle; the imperfect gills few; *taste* and *smell* agreeable; *spores* white.

This Agaric which takes its name from the tree where it is most commonly found, grows also, though less frequently, on the Poplar and Beech. Mr. Berkeley reports it rare; perhaps, however, as it is eminently local, it may here, as in Italy, be common in some places though of unfrequent general occurrence. No country being so rich in Elm-trees as our own, we should probably find *A. ulmarius* more often if the height at which it grows among the branches did not frequently screen it from observation.* Though registered in the Flora of Tunbridge Wells, I have not met with a single specimen of it this autumn.

* "Ce Champignon croît au milieu et vers le sommet de l'arbre, de sorte qu'il n'est pas facile à voir ou à récolter."—*Persoon.*

This Agaric dries well and may be kept (not, however, without losing some of its aroma) for a long time without spoiling; the gills, after a time, assume the same hue as the pileus.

AGARICUS FUSIPES, *Bull.*

Subgenus CLYTOCYBE.   Subdivision CHONDROPODES.

"Il a le même goût que le Champignon de Couche, quoique un peu plus prononcé."—*Persoon.*

Bot. Char. Gregarious; *pileus* fleshy, loose, of a uniform brown colour, sometimes marked with dark blotches, as if burnt; *gills* nearly free, serrated, at first dirty-white, afterwards a clear bistre; easily separable from the stalk; *stalk* hollow, ventricose, sulcate, rooting, spindle-shaped, slightly grooved, tapering at the base, sometimes cracked transversely, varying singularly both in length and breadth.

This excellent fungus is very abundant throughout summer and autumn, coming up in tufts at the roots of old Oak-trees after rain. It may be easily recognized by its peculiar spindle-shaped stalk.

Vittadini does not mention it, nor does its name occur in the list of esculent funguses in the Diz. di Med. Class.; notwithstanding which the young plants make an excellent pickle; while the full-grown ones may be stewed or dressed in any of the usual modes adopted for the common mushroom.

AGARICUS VAGINATUS, *Bull.*

Series 1. LEUCOSPORUS.   Subgenus 1. AMANITA.

"La Coucoumèle grise (*Ag. vag.*) est une des espèces les plus délicates et les plus sûres à manger."—*De Candolle.*

Bot. Char. "Margin of the pileus sulcate, gills white, stuffed with cottony pith, fistulose, attenuated upwards, almost smooth; volva like a sheath. Woods and pastures, August and October; not uncommon. *Pileus* four inches or more broad, plane, slightly depressed in the centre, scarcely umbonate, fleshy, but not at the extreme margin, which is elegantly grooved in consequence, viscid when moist, beautifully glossy when dry; epidermis easily detached, more or less studded with brown scales, the remnants of the volva, not persistent; *gills* free, ventricose, broadest in front, often imbricated, white; *sporules* white, round; *stem* six inches or more high, from half to an inch thick, attenuated upwards, obtuse at the base, furnished with a volva, this adnate below to the extent of an inch, with the base of the stem, closely surrounding it above as in a sheath, but with the margin sometimes expanded; within and at the base marked with the groovings of the pileus, brittle, sericeo-squamulose, scarcely fibrillose, but splitting with ease longitudinally, hollow, or rather stuffed with fine cottony fibres; the very base solid, not acrid, insipid. *Smell* scarcely any. It occurs of various colours, the more general one is a mouse-grey" (*Berkeley*).

The perfect accuracy of the above description will strike every one familiar with this species. Vittadini speaks of it as a solitary fungus, but I have found it on more than one occasion in rings. Its flesh, being very delicate and tender, must not be over-dressed. When properly fried in butter or oil, and as soon after gathering as possible, the *Ag. vaginatus* will be found inferior to but few Agarics in its flavour.

AGARICUS VIOLACEUS, *Linn.*
Subgenus 18. INOLOMA.

Bot. Char. Pileus from four to six inches broad, obtuse, expanded, covered with soft hairs, colour deep violet; *stem* spongy, grey, tinged with violet, minutely downy, about four inches high; *veil* fugacious, composed of fine threads; *gills* deep violet when young, but turning tawny in age; *flesh* thick, juicy.

This is a handsome fungus, not very common, but plentiful where it occurs; it grows in woods, particularly under Pine and Fir trees, and may be dressed either with a white or a brown sauce.

AGARICUS CASTANEUS, *Bull.*
Subgenus 19. DERMOCYBE.

Bot. Char. Pileus slightly fleshy, convex when young, at length umbonate, chestnut colour, from one to three inches broad, glabrous; *gills* rather broad, easily detached from the stem, ventricose, changing from light-purple to a ferruginous hue; *stem* rather thin, from one and a half to three inches long, hollow, silvery, light-lilac or white; *veil* delicate, composed of floccose threads; in *taste*, when raw, it somewhat resembles the *Ag. oreades*, but it has no smell.

This *Agaric* may be distinguished from others by its chestnut or bistre colour; it is probably not uncommon; growing all the summer and autumn in woods, and under trees in meadows. Mr. Berkeley reports it esculent; I have no experience of it.

AGARICUS PIPERATUS, *Scop.*
Subgenus 7. GALORRHEUS.

"Ed è veramente commestibile e saporoso quando se ne levi il latte."
Bendiscioli.

Bot. Char. "*Pileus* infundibuliform, rigid, smooth, white; gills very narrow, close; milk, and the solid blunt stem, white. In woods, July and August. *Pileus* 3–7 inches broad, slightly rugulose, quite smooth, white, a little clouded with umber, or stained with yellow where scratched or bruised, convex, more or less depressed, often quite infundibuliform, more or less waved, fleshy, thick, firm but brittle; margin involute at first, sometimes excentric, milk-white, hot. *Gills* generally very narrow ($\frac{1}{70}$ of an inch broad), but sometimes much broader, cream-colour, repeatedly dichotomous, very close, 'like the teeth of an ivory comb,' decurrent from the shape of the pileus, when bruised changing to umber. *Stem* 1–3 inches high, 1½–2 inches thick, often compressed, minutely pruinose, solid, but spongy within, the substance breaking up into transverse cavities."*

Though very acrid when raw, it loses its bad qualities entirely by cooking, and is extensively used on the Continent, prepared in various ways. It is preserved for winter use by drying or pickling in a mixture of salt and vinegar (*Berkeley*).

I have frequently eaten this fungus at Lucca, where it is very abundant, but as it resembles the *Ag. vellereus* in appearance, with the properties of which we are unacquainted, too much caution cannot be exercised in learning to discriminate it from this and neighbouring species.

* Berkeley.

AGARICUS VIRGINEUS, *Wulf.*
Subgenus 8. CLITOCYBE. Subdivision CAMAROPHYLLI.
White Field-Agaric.

Bot. Char. Pileus from one to **two inches** broad, margin involute when young, then expanded, depressed in the centre. *Gills* deep, connected with veins, sometimes forked, **broadly adnate**, but breaking away from the stem as the pileus becomes depressed. **Stem** six lines broad at the top, tapering downwards, **not** more than **two at the base**; at first **stuffed with fibres**, then **hollow**, excentric; the whole plant white, with occasionally a tinge of **pink**. *Taste* pleasant, odour disagreeable.

These graceful little Agarics grow in pastures, and **are extremely common** in the autumn. They **are so** small that **it** requires a great many of them to make a dish, but as they occur frequently in the same fields with puff-balls, and may be dressed in the same manner, it is not unusual when the **supply** is scarce to serve them together, with the same sauce. The flavour of *Ag.* **virgineus** is not unlike that of *Ag. oreades.*

TUBER ÆSTIVUM, *Vitt.*
PLATE VIII. FIG. 2.

Peridium warty, of a blackish-brown colour, the warts polygonal and **striate, flesh traversed by** numerous veins; **asci** 4–6-spored; **spores** elliptical, reticulated.

This plant, the common truffle of our markets, is abundant in Wiltshire and some other parts **of England, and probably occurs in many** places **where** it escapes **observation, from its subterranean habit.**

CONCLUSION.

Italy is not the country for the English florist; he will find twenty times as many petals at home. Trim parterres are not inventions of the South; summer-houses would be no luxuries in a climate that never knows winter; the only Conservatories that flourish there are not for flowers, but for music. In few northern regions is Flora worse off for a bouquet than at Rome or Naples; regarded merely as the herald of Spring and not appreciated for her own sake, as soon as she has waved her wand over the land and covered it with the March blossoms of Crocuses, Cyclamens, and Anemones, her reign is over. All scents are held in equal abhorrence save those of frankincense and garlic, for which there seems to be a prescriptive toleration; but every other odour, fetid or fragrant, musk* or mignonette, is equally proscribed; and an Italian Signora would as soon permit a Locusta to cook for her, as a violet to scent her boudoir. To pick wild flowers is as dangerous as it is difficult to find cultivated ones; a *coup de soleil* or a fever is easily procured by imprudent exposure before sunset, while the interval between

---

* In 1843, the friends of a patient, for whom I had occasion to prescribe some musk, had recourse to many chemists in succession before the licensed dealer in it could be found, and he was obliged by law to keep it in his back premises.

that and night is too brief to be employed for the purpose;
but when the season for flowers is long past, and Autumn
with her fruits is come round again, when the stranger can
wander forth where he lists without an umbrella, he will be
able to luxuriate amidst the lovely scenery, and to delight
himself in the natural history of the district: the season of
the periodical rains has ceased; the repose of the forest is no
longer troubled by the Power of the waters; the mountain
Pines borne for miles down into the valleys are stranded on
the broad shingly bed of the exhausted torrent; broken
bridges are safely repaired; the maize is receiving the last
mellowing touches as it festoons the cottage fronts, the
prickly chestnut-pods are beginning to gape and the brown
chestnuts to leap out shining from their envelopes; the last re-
luctant olive has been beaten from the bough; the vintage has
nearly ceased to bleed; night fires* already begin to flicker on
the mountains, and the hemp stubble is daily crackling on
the plain. This is indeed the time for enjoying Italy; nature
has revived again, and with nature, man. The feverish torpor,
I had almost ventured to call it the summer hybernation, has
ceased with September, and Autumn has come round with
the vivifying influence of a new Spring; then if we go abroad
to wander, whether our walk be across plains or through up-
land woods, we shall not stroll a mile without stopping a
hundred times to admire what is to many of us a nearly new
class of objects which have sprung up suddenly and now beset
our path on every side. These are the Fungus tribe, which
are as beautiful as the fairest flowers, and more useful than

---

* Night fires. This is to clear the ground under the Chestnut-trees for the falling fruits, which might otherwise be lost amidst the heath. But the practice is unsafe; as many a tree has been charred by the flames, and some have actually taken fire and given rise to a general conflagration.

most fruits; and now that butchers' meat is bad, that the beans have become stringy, and the potatoes are hydrated by the rain, they appear thus opportunely to eke out the scantiness of autumnal larders in the South and give a fresh zest to the daily repast. Well may their sudden apparition surprise us, for not ten days since the waters were all out, and only three or four nights back peals of thunder rattled against the casements and kept the most determined sleepers in awful vigil; and now—behold the meadows by natural magic studded with countless fairy-rings of every diameter, formed of such species as grow upon the ground, while the Chestnut and the Oak are teeming with a new class of fruits that had no previous blossoming, many of which have already attained their full growth. We recollect with gratitude the objects of a pursuit, which has accidentally brought us to such an acquaintance with the diversities of Italian scenery as we never should have experienced without it. In fishing, it is not the fish we catch, which alone repays us for our toil; it is the wandering as the rivulet wanders, "at its own sweet will," the exercise and the appetite consequent upon it, the prize in natural history, the reciting aloud, or reflecting as we walk, and when it is pleasantly warm the "molles sub arbore somni," which console us for the lack of sport. On the same principle, mushroom-hunting may be recommended to the young naturalist not only for the beauty of the objects which he is sure to come upon (if he do but hunt at the right season), but also because in that most beautiful of months, whether at home or abroad, it brings the wanderer out of beaten paths to fall in with many striking views which he would not otherwise have explored. The extremely limited time during which funguses are to be found, their fragility, their infinite diversity, their ephemeral existence, these, too, add to the interest of an autumnal walk in quest of them. At Lucca, leaving idleness and indigestion in bed, just as the sun was beginning to shoot his first rays on the white convents and the spires of the village churches on the mountains, making morning above, while the deep valley beneath was still in twilight, it was pleasant to pass the little opening coffee-house with its two or three candidates for early breakfast, and crossing the noiseless trout-stream over the little bridge, to enter one of those old chestnut-forests and begin clambering up the laddery pathway, to reach the summit just as he poured his full effulgence on the magnificent rival of the Lucchese and Modenese territories. Pleasant, too, was it on the road Romeward, pausing a few days to enjoy the exquisite scenery about Spoleto, to climb the steep streets to the cathedral, and thence, passing the giddy viaduct several hundred feet above the white ravine which it traverses, to issue upon those Nursian Hills then fragrant with the breath of morning, "le beau matin qui sort humide et pâle," and with the scent of sweet herbs; but above all other hills renowned for the fragrance of those everreproductive mines of coal-black subterranean truffles! It is a pleasant remembrance to have plucked the crimson Amanite, that ministered to a Cæsar's decease, in the very neighbourhood of the Palatine Hill; to have collected mushrooms amidst the meadows of Horace's farm, where he tells us they grew best; and to have watched along the moist pastures of the Cremera a stand of the stately *Ag. procerus* nodding upon their stalks; or, standing on the heights above Sorrento, just as the setting sun flashed upon the waters of the bay ere they engulfed him, and left us to his sister the evening star, to have come upon that wonderful *Polyporus tuberaster* whose matrix is the hard stone, from which it derives strength and luxuriance as if from a soft and genial soil.

But not only in Italy, in our own country also, the Collector in Mycology will have to traverse much beautiful and diversified scenery; amid woods, greenswards, winding lanes, rich meadows, healthy commons, open downs, the nodding hop-grove and the mountain sheep-path; and all shone upon by an autumnal sunset,—as compared with Southern climes "obscurely bright," and unpreceded by that beautiful rosy tint which bathes the whole landscape in Italy, but with a far finer background of clouds to reflect its departed glories: and throughout all this range of scenery he will never hunt in vain; indulgent gamekeepers, made aware of what he is poaching, may warn him that he is not collecting mushrooms, but will never warn him off from the best-kept preserves. In such rambles he will see, what I have this autumn (1847) myself witnessed, whole *hundredweights of rich wholesome diet rotting under the trees; woods teeming with food and not one hand to gather it;* and this, perhaps, in the midst of potato blight, poverty and all manner of privations, and public prayers against imminent famine. I have indeed grieved, when I reflected on the straitened condition of the lower orders this year, to see pounds innumerable of extempore beef-steaks growing on our oaks in the shape of *Fistulina hepatica*; *Ag. fusipes* to pickle, in clusters under them; Puffballs, which some of our friends have not inaptly compared to sweet-bread for the rich delicacy of their unassisted flavour; *Hydna* as good as oysters, which they somewhat resemble in taste; *Agaricus deliciosus*, reminding us of tender lamb-kidneys; the beautiful yellow Chantarelle, that *kalon kagathon* of diet, growing by the bushel, and no basket but our own to pick up a few specimens in our way; the sweet nutty-flavoured *Boletus*, in vain calling himself *edulis* where there was none to believe him; the dainty *Orcella*; the *Ag. heterophyllus*,

which tastes like the craw-fish when grilled; the *Ag. ruber* and *Ag. virescens*, to cook in any way, and equally good in all;—these were among the most conspicuous of the *trouvailles*. But that the reader may know all he is likely to find in one single autumn, let him glance at the catalogue below.*
He may at first alarm his friends' cooks, but their fears will, I promise him, soon be appeased, after one or two trials of this new class of viands, and he will not long pass either for a conjuror or something worse, in giving directions to stew *toadstools*. As soon as he is initiated in this class of dainties, he will, I am persuaded, lose no time in making the discovery known to the poor of the neighbourhood; while in so doing he will render an important service to the country at large, by instructing the indigent and ignorant in the choice of an ample, wholesome, and excellent article, which they may convert into money, or consume at their own tables, when properly prepared, throughout the winter.

* The whole of the species mentioned in the annexed list were met with by the author this summer and autumn (1847), and partaken of by himself and friends, viz. *Amanita vaginata*; *Ag. rubescens, procerus, prunulus, ruber, heterophyllus, virescens, deliciosus, nebularis, **personatus**, virgineus, fusipes, oreades, ostreatus, Orcella, campestris* (and its varieties *edulis* and *pratensis*), *exquisitus, comatus*, and *ulmarius*; *Cantharellus cibarius*; **Polyporus** *frondosus*; *Boletus edulis* and *scaber*; **Fistulina** *hepatica*; **Hydnum** *repandum*; *Helvella lacunosa*; *Peziza* acetabulum and *Bovista plumbea*; *Lycoperdon gemmatum* and *Clavaria strigosa*.

NOTE ON THE ARRANGEMENT OF THE SPORES IN HYMENOMYCETOUS FUNGUSES.

On the authority of Link, Fries, Vittadini, and other Continental mycologists, I have, in speaking of the spores of the genera *Agaricus*, *Boletus*, *Cantharellus*, *Hydnum*, and *Clavaria*, represented them as enclosed in cases (thecæ or sporanges). But from an interesting memoir, published by Mr. Berkeley in the 'Annals of Natural History,' "On the Fructification of the Pileate and Clavate tribes of Hymenomycetous Fungi," which I had not then perused, it would appear that this arrangement only holds good with respect to *Pezizas*, *Helvellas*, and *Morels*, and not with respect to the above-mentioned genera, the spores of which are attached (generally in a quaternary and star form) to the ends of tubes, to which Mr. Berkeley has given the name of *sporophores*; a disposition which, as he observes, had been long ago pointed out by the great Florentine mycologist, Micheli. M. Montagne, in his 'Recherches Anatomiques et Physiologiques sur l'Hymenium,' while he confirms the fact of a quaternary disposition of the spores in general, thinks that during the *first* stage of their development they are lodged *within* the sporiferous tubes, to the mouths of which they afterwards adhere by means of short spiculæ or branchlets.

These, like all other questions connected with the minute reproductive granules of funguses, require for their solution not only the most dexterous manipulation and the aid of the finest modern microscopes, but are likely even then to exercise the ingenuity of the curious.

THE END.

JOHN EDWARD TAYLOR, PRINTER,
LITTLE QUEEN STREET, LINCOLN'S INN FIELDS.

W Fitch, del et lith.
Vincent Brooks, Imp

Pl. II.

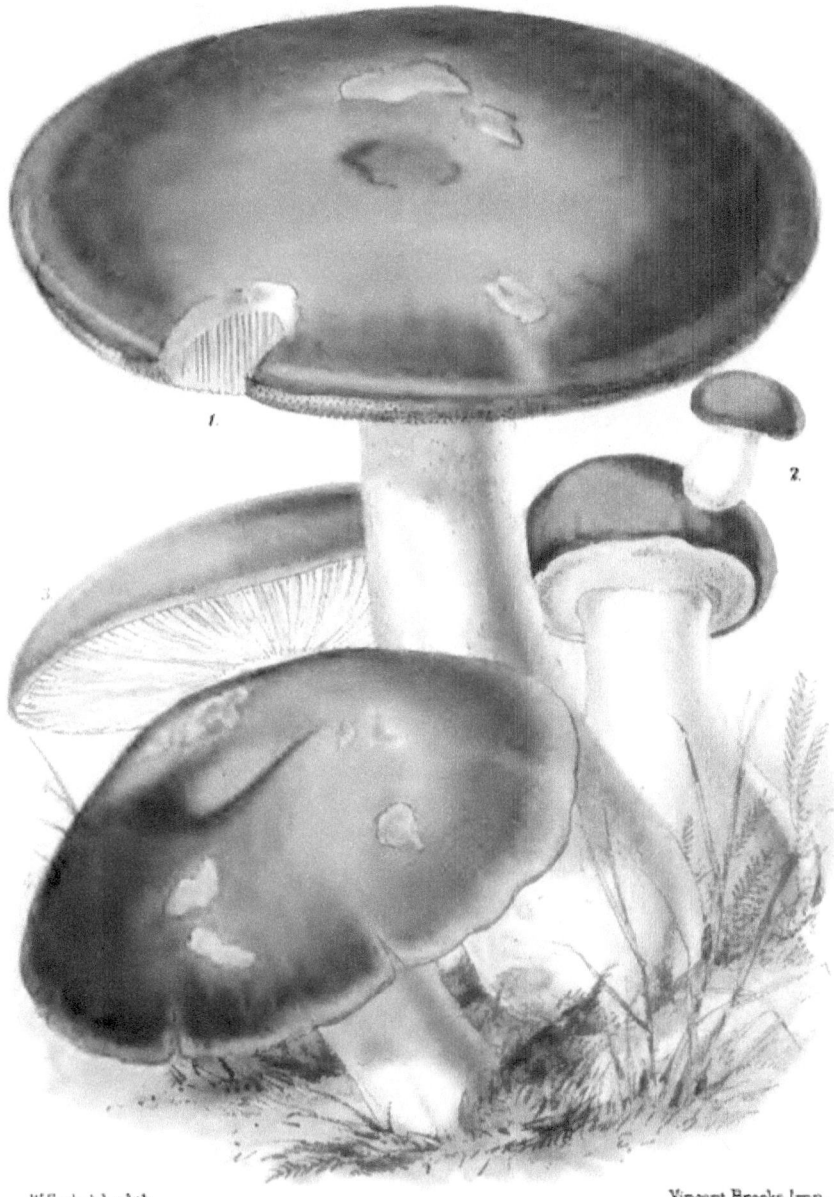

W. Fitch del et lith.   Vincent Brooks, Imp.

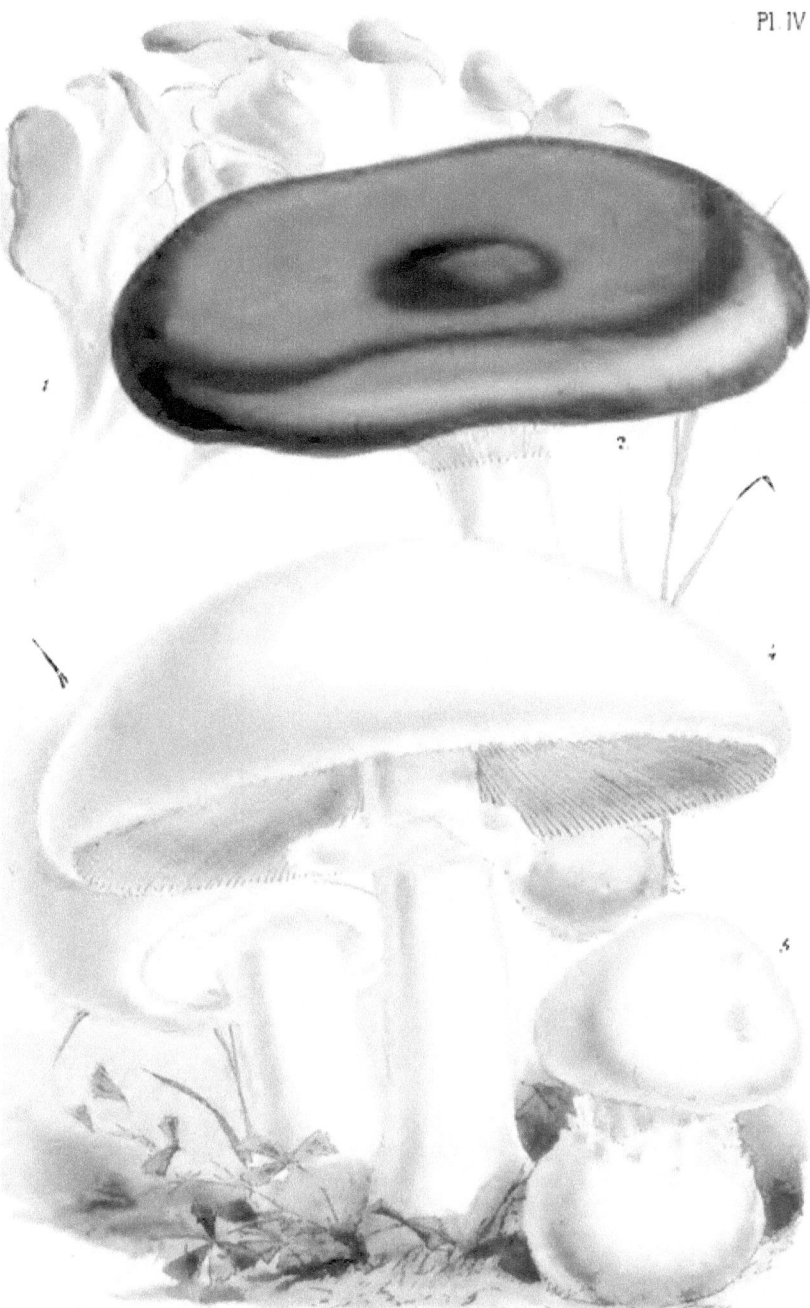

Pl. IV

W Fitch del et lith. Vincent Brooks, Imp.

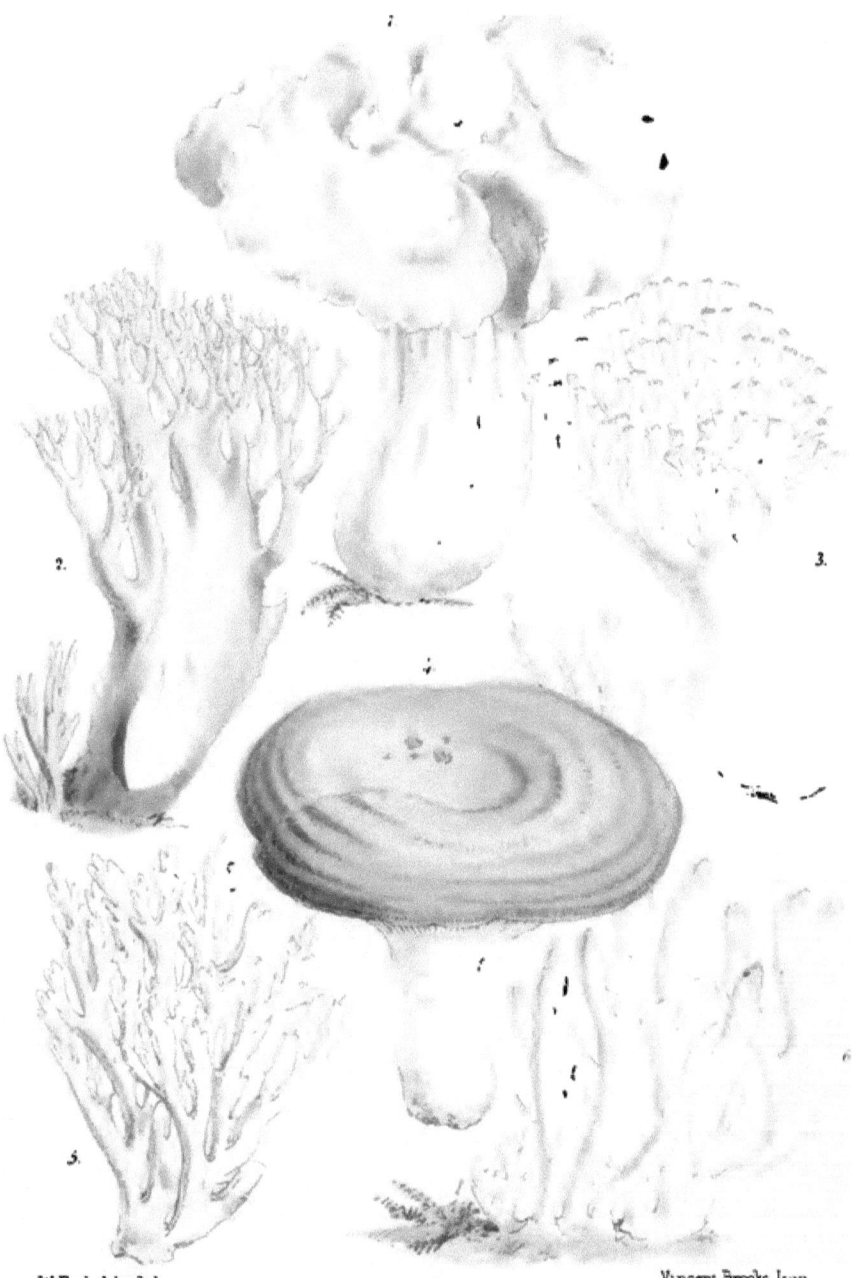

W Fitch, del et lith. Vincent Brooks, Imp

W Fitch, del et lith. Vincent Brooks, Imp.

Pl. VIII

W. Fitch, del et lith.

Vincent Brooks, Imp.

Pl IX

Vincent Brooks, Imp

W. Fitch del. et lith.   Vincent Brooks, Imp.

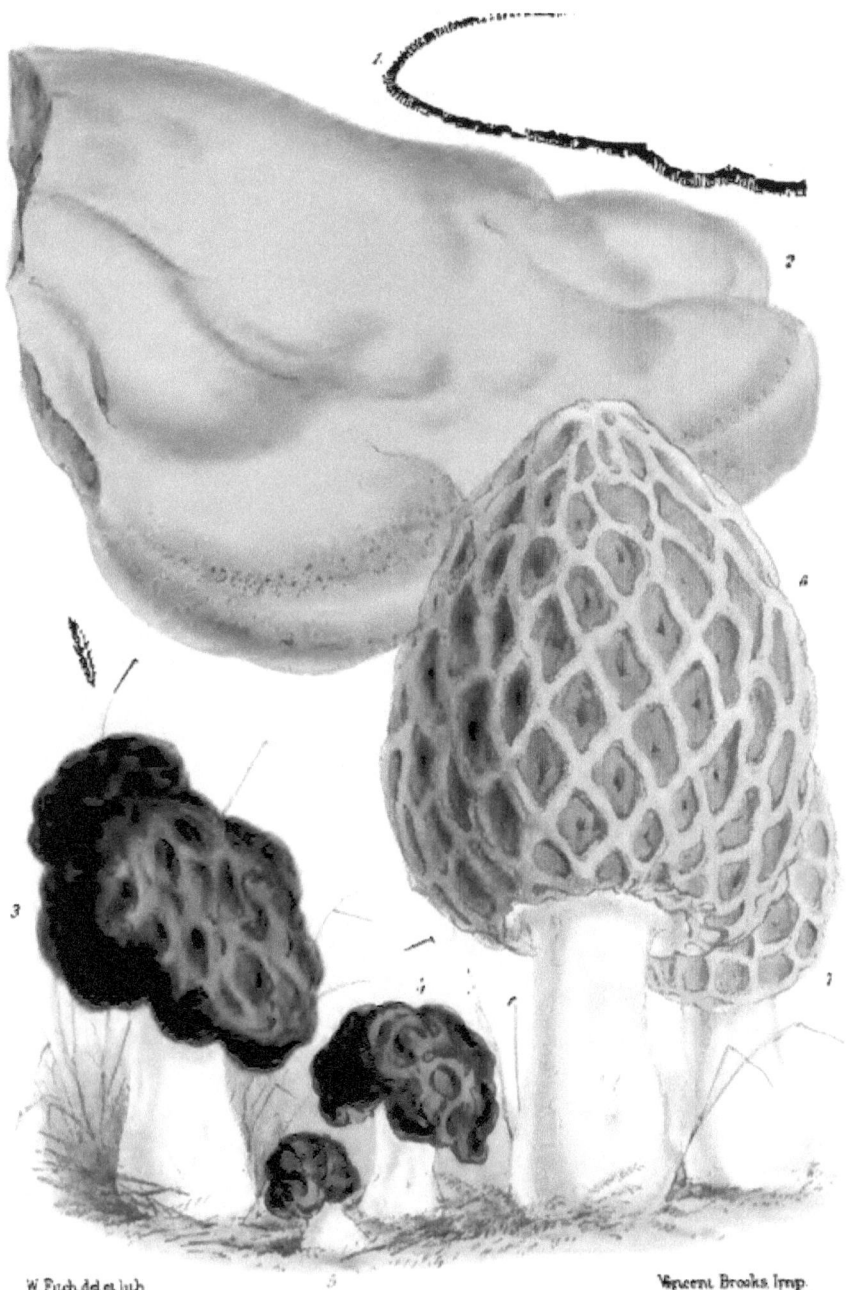

W. Fitch del et lith.
Vincent Brooks, Imp.

www.ingramcontent.com/pod-product-compliance
Lightning Source LLC
Chambersburg PA
CBHW020240170426
43202CB00008B/156